Time Out

Barcelona
Eating & Drinking

timeout.com/barcelona

Penguin Books

PENGUIN BOOKS

Published by the Penguin Group
Penguin Books Ltd, 80 Strand, London WC2R ORL, England
Penguin Books USA Inc., 375 Hudson Street, New York, New York 10014, USA
Penguin Books Australia Ltd, 250 Camberwell Road, Camberwell, Victoria 3124,
Australia
Penguin Books Canada Ltd, 10 Alcorn Avenue, Toronto, Ontario, Canada M4V 3B2
Penguin Books (NZ) Ltd, cnr Rosedale and Airborne Roads, Albany, Auckland, New
Zealand

Penguin Books Ltd, Registered Offices: Harmondsworth, Middlesex, England

First published 2002
10 9 8 7 6 5 4 3 2 1

Colour reprographics by Icon, Crowne House, 56-58 Southwark Street, London
SE1 1UN
Printed and bound by Cayfosa-Quebecor, Ctra. de Caldes, Km 3 08 130 Sta,
Perpètua de Mogoda, Barcelona, Spain

Edited and designed by
Time Out Guides Limited
Universal House
251 Tottenham Court Road
London W1T 7AB
Tel + 44 (0)20 7813 3000
Fax + 44 (0)20 7813 6001
Email guides@timeout.com
www.timeout.com

Editorial
Editor Sally Davies
Deputy Editor Casilda Grigg
Listings Editor Nuria Rodriguez
Maps Editor John O'Donovan
Proofreader Tamsin Shelton

Editorial Director Peter Fiennes
Series Editor Sarah Guy
Guides Co-ordinator Anna Norman

Design
Group Art Director John Oakey
Art Director Mandy Martin
Art Editor Scott Moore
Designers Benjamin de Lotz, Sarah Edwards, Lucy Grant
Picture Editor Kerri Miles
Deputy Picture Editor Kit Burnet
Picture Librarian Sarah Roberts
Scanning & Imaging Dan Conway
Ad make-up Glen Impey

Advertising
Group Commercial Director Lesley Gill
Sales Director Mark Phillips
International Sales Co-ordinator Ross Canadé
Advertisement Sales (Barcelona)
Samantha Lhoas
Advertising Assistant Sabrina Ancilleri

Administration
Chairman Tony Elliott
Managing Director Mike Hardwick
Group Financial Director Kevin Ellis
Group General Manager Nichola Coulthard
Marketing Director Christine Cort
Marketing Manager Mandy Martinez
Production Manager Mark Lamond
Production Controller Samantha Furniss
Accountant Sarah Bostock

Features in this guide were written and researched by Sally Davies (*Eating in Barcelona*); Susan Low (*Wines of Catalonia*). **Boxes were written by** Jonathan Bennett (*La Boqueria, Takeaways*); Sally Davies (*Riding the new wave, Out of town, Slices of life, Say cheese, Jamón jamón*); Nadia Feddo (*Teashops*); Nick Chapman (*Pub crawl*); Jeffrey Swartz (*Olives in Catalonia, Food festivals*).

Restaurant reviews were written by Sally Davies and Nadia Feddo, along with Jonathan Bennett, Amy Egan, Jeffrey Swartz. **Cafés and bars were reviewed by** Amber Ockrassa, along with John O'Donovan and Nick Chapman.

The Editor would like to thank all the contributors, as well as David Noguer, Jeanine Beck, Jenny Brickman and everyone else who sent in suggestions. Time Out would like to thank Ruth Jarvis.

Maps by JS Graphics john@jsgraphics.co.uk

Photography by Xavier Cervera, Oriol Tarridas and Ingrid Morato except pages 14, 15, 17, 18, provided by the featured establishments.

Contents

About the guide

The reviews in this guide are based solely on the experiences of *Time Out* restaurant reviewers. All the restaurants, bars and cafés listed here were visited anonymously over a period of a few months, and *Time Out* footed the bills. No payment of any kind from restaurant owners has secured or influenced a review in this guide.

In the listings, the times given are those observed by the kitchen; in other words, the times within which one is fairly certain to be able to sit down and order a meal. These can change according to the time of year and the owners' whims. It is often a good idea to call ahead (although that's easier if you speak a little Spanish or Catalan). Average prices listed are per person for three courses, excluding service, wine and other extras. Average prices have been graded on the following scale:

up to €20	€
€20 to €30	€€
€30 to €45	€€€
over €45	€€€€

We list the credit cards accepted by the restaurant or bar by initials: AmEx (American Express), DC (Diners Club), MC (MasterCard) and V (Visa).

The star system is there to help you identify top performers at a glance. A red star ★ beside the name of a restaurant means that our reviewers found it to be one of the best in the city.

Eating
in Barcelona

A rough-hewn slice of country bread, smeared with a tomato ripened in the Mediterranean sun and a trickle of sweet, fruity olive oil, served with a hunk of sheep's cheese, some good jamón serrano and a jug of lusty red – there are few meals as simple or as satisfying, and none as essentially Catalan. No amount of Pacific Rim cuisine, designer tapas, nouvelle artistry or imported exotica can ever match the pleasure that this kind of lunch can bring, but should you be after some occasional variety, there has never been such an abundance of choice.

Immigration and tourism have had a considerable impact on what Barcelona has to offer, as has a growing international awareness of one of the most historically important cuisines of the world. The latest crop of Spanish superchefs, traditionally a Basque phenomenon, has emerged from Catalan soil, which in turn has awakened gourmet interest. Celebrity cookery books fly off the shelves, and cookery schools can't cope with the demand from wannabe chefs. In recent years, the explosion in the

SAN MARZANO®

number of places to eat and drink in Barcelona – over 4,000 at the last count – has been unprecedented. In this guide we have tried not only to highlight some of the best but also to dish the dirt on those places which are firm fixtures on the tourist trail but are all too often trading on a reputation earned in days gone by.

WHAT AND WHERE

Catalan cuisine, with its rich, stewy dishes, pungent sauces and unexpected combinations – lobster with chicken, prawns with rabbit – still dominates, along with a host of places specialising in food from other Spanish regions; the Basque Country in particular, but also Galicia, La Rioja, Castile, and to a lesser extent the Balearics and Andalucia. Slowly international cuisine is starting to take hold, but it should be said that not all of it is truly authentic; unaccustomed local palates and the difficulty of sourcing key ingredients mean that it can be difficult to find really good Indian, say, or Italian, food. Middle Eastern and Japanese restaurants have been rather more successful, along with a growing number of Latin American places. The other trend creeping inexorably (and perhaps regrettably) into Spanish culture, is that of the fusion restaurant. Here it pays to think long and hard before eating in smaller, cheaper restaurants, where cooks are unlikely to have the experience or training to turn out dishes from Thailand, Japan, Mexico and Italy with equal panache.

Apart from the Pakistani restaurants which abound in the Raval, most of the ethnic variety is to be found in Gràcia.

Japanese restaurants, being relatively expensive, are mainly found in the Eixample or Zona Alta, where most of the top-end restaurants are, while seafood restaurants, for the most part, are in and around Barceloneta and the ports (with some notable exceptions). Catalan restaurants are evenly spread throughout the city, as is the impressive variety of vegetarian restaurants.

Bars and cafés are not so bound by type/area; but loosely speaking, the dressier bars will be in the Eixample and Zona Alta, while those in the Raval tend to be more bohemian; Gràcia nightlife has a studenty feel, and most of the heavily touristed places are around the ports and in the Barri Gòtic. The area known as the Born, in La Ribera (Born and La Ribera are often used synonymously), is currently enjoying very fashionable status, and has a stack of trendy bars to show for it.

Anyone hoping to spend their time tapeando (loosely, tapas-hopping) in Barcelona is going to be disappointed; there just isn't the wealth of tapas bars found in cities in other parts of Spain. Apart from a few huge tapas barns up on Passeig de Gràcia, and the old-style tascas (tapas bars) on C/Mercè in the Barri Gòtic, the best option is Basque bars, where they serve pintxos (*see pp80-81*, **Snack attack**).

HOW

Dining out in Barcelona, you may occasionally feel hurried – often the pudding menu appears on the table before the main course has been cleared – but this is a reflection of the local tendency to rattle through courses; any lingering tends to be done afterwards, with coffee and brandy. In cheaper restaurants, it's also not unusual for waiters to bring out dishes as they are ready, so you may get your main course while someone else at your table is still on their starter, or you might even find two courses put in front of you at once.

In most bars and cafés, the form is generally to pay at the end. Exceptions to this are late-night places and those with a lot of tourists, who, presumably, are not to be trusted. Anywhere with pavement tables or a terrace is likely to use a 'pay-as-you-go' system, and it's worth noting, too, that you are often charged more if you sit outside.

WHEN

Catalans eat late: lunch starts around 2pm and goes on until about 3.30 or 4pm, and dinner is served from 9pm until about 11.30pm or midnight. Some restaurants open earlier in the evening, but arriving before 9.30 or 10pm generally means you will be dining alone or in the company of foreign tourists. Reserving a table is generally a good idea, especially on Friday and Saturday nights. Most restaurants close on Sunday evenings and those that do not fill up quickly. Many also close for lengthy holidays, including about a week off over Easter, two or three weeks in August or early September, and often the first week in January. Annual closures of more than two weeks are listed where possible, but it's always a good idea to call ahead in holiday periods just to be sure.

PRICES AND PAYMENT

The price guidelines we have used in this book are indications of the cost of an average starter, main course and dessert – not including wine, service or cover charge. € is used for anything under €20; €€ for €20-30; €€€ for €30-45, and €€€€ means the average meal will set you

back over €45. Eating out in Barcelona is not as cheap as it used to be, but low mark-ups on wine keep the cost relatively low for Northern Europeans and Americans. All but the upmarket restaurants are required by law to serve an economical fixed-price menú (not to be confused with the menu, which is la carta) at lunchtime – usually consisting of a starter, main course, dessert, bread and something to drink. The idea is to provide cheaper meals for the workers, and while it can be a real bargain, it is not by any means a taster menu or a showcase for the chef's greatest hits. The menú del día (also sometimes called the menú turístico, as it was originally dreamed up by Franco to attract tourists in the 1960s) tends to repeat the same

basic and universally acceptable dishes day in, day out –
which may mean nothing more than a very basic salad,
followed by fried chicken and chips, with a yoghurt or piece
of fruit for dessert. There are, of course, exceptions to this;
we have tried to highlight those restaurants that are better
than average.

Laws governing the issue of prices are routinely flouted,
but legally, menus must declare if the seven per cent IVA
(VAT) is included in prices or not (it rarely is), and also if
there is a cover charge (which is generally expressed as a
charge for bread). Waiters in Spain earn a respectable
salary, so tipping tends to be a matter of a couple of euros,
rather than the 10% expected elsewhere.

Wines
of Catalonia

PENEDÈS

1 + 1 = 3

If you turn your back to the Mediterranean, all roads from Barcelona lead to wine country. And it's not just any wine country; the vineyards of Catalonia produce some of the best – and most expensive – wines in Spain. Take the motorway south-west out of the city and after an hour or so, suburbia gives way to green, vine-clad hills and plains. This is the Penedès, one of the largest wine-growing regions in Catalonia, and one that until recently was virtually synonymous with one wine: cava. These days the Penedès' repute extends to its deeply coloured reds and a growing number of still white wines, in addition to its famous sparkler.

Quite how a single region can produce such a vast range of styles seems a mystery until you see the land itself; the terrain varies enormously, thanks to the mitigating influence of the hills. Everyday drinking wines, white (blanc in Catalan, blanco in Spanish), red (negre/tinto) and rosé

(rosat/rosado) are made in the warm, low-lying region of the Baix Penedès. In the highest vineyards (the Alt Penedès), cool weather-loving varieties such as riesling, pinot noir, chardonnay and gewürztraminer hold sway. The middle reaches of the region are where most of the cava comes from, although red wines made from quality French grape varieties such as cabernet sauvignon and merlot, as well as the Spanish tempranillo, are made here too.

Although Catalans have long been dedicated to their native sparkling wine, cava is still considered by many non-Catalans to be poor man's champagne. In fact, quality has improved in recent years, and well-made cava is often more pleasurable to the palate than bog-standard champagne. Part of the reason behind the rise in quality is that many top producers have been taking part in a little French-inspired jiggery-pokery. They sneak some chardonnay and pinot noir (the main grapes used to make champagne) into the traditional blend of Catalan grape varieties. It's all completely legal, but there have been the inevitable bouts of moral outrage amid cries of untraditional. Nevertheless, cavas with the richness and roundness of these French varieties are simply more appealing to international palates than the earthier traditional styles. Cavas, old and new-style, to watch for include Albet i Noya, Juvé & Camps, Mascaró, Raventós i Blanc and Jaume Serra, as well as the big names, Codorníu and Freixenet.

Cava aside, the Penedès is now noted among the vinoscenti as a producer of top-flight red wines. The prime mover behind this switch to red is the respected Catalan winemaker Miguel Torres. A pioneer of Spain's vinous new wave, Torres was among the first to start working with international grape varieties – cabernet sauvignon, chardonnay, merlot and the like – way back in the mid 1960s. He was also among the first to drive home the important message that quality counts. While most producers in the country stuck to their traditional winemaking methods, producing basic plonk for ordinary glugging, Torres was among the first to spot and exploit the region's potential. He's also the biggest advocate of native Catalan varieties, which makes him as popular at home as he is abroad. Other good producers include Jean León (now owned by Torres) and Masía Bach.

Over the past decade, the Catalan wine region to make the biggest headlines in Spain and elsewhere is Priorat. As recently as the mid 1980s, the future of this little comarca (district) 80 kilometres (50 miles) west of Barcelona was

looking pretty dismal. This austere land of steep hillsides and wizened vegetation had been in decline since the 19th century, when phylloxera wiped out the majority of European vineyards. Following the infestation, many farmers left the region. The hardships involved in making wine in this often inhospitable climate were hardly a draw for the younger generation, many of whom moved to the cities for an easier life.

The turnaround from doomed to in-demand has been dramatic. Thanks to the vision of a group of pioneering young winemakers, Priorat is now home to some of the most exciting – and priciest – wines in the world. For wine buffs, names like L'Ermita, Clos Mogador and Finca Dofí are among the holiest of the holies, lusted after by well-heeled wine collectors and restaurateurs the world over. The red garnacha grape is king in Priorat; here the vines outperform those in just about every other region or country that grows the variety.

Part of the reason for the success of Priorat wines is the region's unusual terrain. The high altitude, steep hillsides and the strange black and gold slate soil, called llicorella in Catalan, combine to make concentrated, impressively fleshy, spice and herb-inflected wines. Producers to watch for include Álvaro Palacios (who makes L'Ermita and Finca Dofí), Costers del Siurana, Mas Martinet, René Barbier, Cellers de Scala Dei, Masía Barril and Masía Duch.

The quality revolution is blazing its way across Catalonia, slowly in some parts, more rapidly in others. Although the Tarragona region, south-west of the Penedès, continues to drag its feet, wines from Falset, a small comarca within that region, are taking the call to quality seriously; it's an area to keep an eye on. Another place to watch is the Costers del Segre region west of Barcelona. Here a couple of producers, Raïmat and Castell del Remei, have more than proved the value of the vineyard land, thanks to a bit of clever irrigation.

Terra Alta, yet further south-west from Tarragona, has the potential – still largely untapped – to produce good wines. Wines from the tiny Alella region, north of Barcelona, are variable, and urban spillover from the city is encroaching on vineyard land here. Empurdà-Costa Brava, up near the

French border, and Pla de Bages, north-west of Barcelona, have yet to awaken from winemaking somnambulance and seldom make interesting drinking.

Nevertheless, there's plenty of the good stuff on offer in Barcelona's bars and restaurants. As in France, regionalism is alive and well in Spain, perhaps even more so in proud Catalonia, which means that you'll have ample opportunity to try the local wines – but if it's Aussie chardonnay and California cabernet you're after, you'll be out of luck. Another plus is the prices; anyone used to the swingeing mark-ups in restaurants elsewhere will find the prices of Barcelona's bottles much easier to swallow.

This being a wine-producing region, you'll find little of the wine snobbery that often reigns in restaurants and wine bars at home. Wine is a pleasure, not a cerebral exercise. Don't be surprised to see bar-goers knocking back jugs of standard white, red and rosé, sometimes mixed with water

or lemonade to cut the acidity. (Try doing that in Britain or the US and staying fashionable.) A local speciality is vinos de aguja, wines with very fine bubbles – more like a gentle spritz on the tongue than a full-blown sparkler – these work well as a palate cleanser for oily or fried dishes. Fancier restaurants take a more serious approach to wine, but you'll see few of the tastevin-wearing sommeliers who regard the humiliation of customers as a sport.

As in the French wine-producing regions, Catalan food and Catalan wine have traditionally worked well together. However, the tentacles of influence of überchef Ferran Adrià and his disciples, with their love of numerous small dishes and fixation with pairing surreal ingredients and science-lab techniques on the same plate, can make finding suitable wines seem like a quest for the Holy Grail. The best tack is to do as the Catalans do – sit back, have a drink and enjoy the experience, no matter how bizarre.

Visit a vineyard

Many of Catalonia's vineyards are open to visitors, although it is a good idea to book ahead.

Can Soniol del Castell

Masía Grabuac, Ctra de Vilafranca a Font Rubí (BV2127) km 6, Font Rubí (93 897 84 26). **Open** by appointment.
A limited quantity of very fine cava is made at this vineyard, centred on a historic masía.

Caves Codorníu

Avda Codorníu, Sant Sadurní d'Anoia (93 818 32 32). **Open** 9am-5pm Mon-Fri; 9am-1pm Sat, Sun. **Admission** free Mon-Fri; €1.50 Sat, Sun.
Tour includes a short film, a mini-train ride through the cellars and a tasting.

Caves Freixenet

C/Joan Sala 2, Sant Sadurní d'Anoia (93 891 70 00). **Tours** 10am, 11.30am, 3.30pm, 5pm Mon-Thur; 10am, 11.30am Fri. **Admission** free.

Scala Dei

Rambla de la Cartoixa, Scala Dei (977 82 70 27). **Open** by appointment. **Admission** free.
A 12th-century monastery. Great reds, in particular the Cartoixa Scala Dei.

Torres

Finca El Maset, Pacs del Penedès (93 817 74 87/ www.torres.es). **Open** 9am-5pm Mon-Fri; 9am-6pm Sat; 9am-1pm Sun. Tours on the hour. **Admission** free.

Another with a short film, train ride and tour of the cellars, followed by a glass of cava.

Getting there

Alella *By bus* Autocars Casas (93 798 11 00) from corner of Gran Via and C/Roger de Flor. *By car* NII north to Montgat, then left turn to Alella (15km/9 miles).
Alt Penedès *By car* A2, then A7 to Sant Sadurní (44km/27 miles) and Vilafranca (55km/34 miles), or A2, then toll-free N340 from Molins de Rei, which is much slower. *By train* RENFE from Sants or Plaça Catalunya; trains leave hourly 6am-10pm (journey time 45mins). Torres and Cordorníu are a taxi ride from Vilafranca and Sant Sadurní.
Falset, Scala Dei & Gandesa *By car* A2, then A7 to Reus, and right on to N420 for Falset (143km/89 miles) and Gandesa (181km/112 miles). For Scala Dei take T710 from Falset, then turn right at La Vilella Baixa. *By train* RENFE from Sants/Passeig de Gràcia to Marçà-Falset. Six trains daily (2hrs). For Gandesa continue to Mora d'Ebre (20mins) and catch a local bus.

Tourist information

Falset Avda Catalunya 6 (977 83 10 23);
Gandesa Avda Catalunya (977 42 06 14);
Sant Sadurní d'Anoia Plaça de l'Ajuntament 1, baixos (93 891 12 12); **Vilafranca del Penedès** C/Cort 14 (93 892 03 58).

Where to...

EAT LATE

Barri Gòtic
Els Quatre Gats
La Verònica

La Ribera
El Celler de Macondo
Comerç 24
Habana Vieja
Peps Bufet
Pla de la Garsa
Rodrigo
Sikkim
Teranga

Raval
La Fragua
La Gardunya
Lupino
Mama Café

Gràcia
Botafumeiro
Cantina Machito
Figaro
La Gavina
El Glop
Habibi

Eixample
La Tramoia

Ports & Shoreline
Salamanca
Set Portes

DINE AL FRESCO

Barri Gòtic
Café de l'Acadèmia
Les Quinze Nits
El Salón
Taxidermista
La Verònica

La Ribera
Casa Delfin
Café de la Ribera
El Celler de Macondo
Al Passatore
Teranga

Raval
La Fragua

Gràcia
La Buena Tierra
Roig Robí

Ports & Shoreline
Agua
Can Majó
Can Ramonet
El Rebujito de Moncho's
Salamanca
El Suquet de l'Almirall
Xiringuito Escribà

Poble Sec & Sants
La Parra

Horta & Poblenou
Can Travi Nou
Gaig
Els Pescadors

Zona Alta
La Balsa
Tram-Tram
La Venta

DRINK AL FRESCO

Barri Gòtic
L'Antiquari
Bar del Pi
Bilbao-Berria
Bliss
Café d'Estiu
Café Zurich
Glaciar

La Ribera

Café del Born
L'Hivernacle
Suau
Tèxtil Café
La Vinya del Senyor

Raval

Bar Kasparo
Bar Mendizábal
Bar Ra
Horiginal
Iposa Bar
Rita Blue
Els Tres Tombs

Gràcia

Café del Sol
Casa Quimet
Sol Soler
Sureny
Virreina Bar

Eixample

Café Torino
Cervecería Catalana
La Gran Bodega
La Pedrera de Nit
Valor Chocolatería

Ports & Shoreline

Café & Café
Can Ganassa
Jai-ca
Luz de Gas en Port Vell
La Miranda del Museu

Poble Sec & Sants

Bar Primavera
Fundació Miró

Horta & Poblenou

L'Esquinica

Zona Alta

Merbeyé
Mirablau
Partycular

EAT SEAFOOD

La Ribera

Cal Pep
Mundial Bar
Passadis del Pep

Raval

Casa Leopoldo

Gràcia

Botafumeiro

Ports & Shoreline

Can Majó
Can Maño
Can Solé
Can Ramonet
Salamanca
Set Portes
El Suquet de l'Almirall
Xiringuitó Escribà

Poble Sec & Sants

Peixerot

TAKE THE KIDS

Barri Gòtic

The Bagel Shop
El Bosc de les Fades
Los Caracoles
Mesón Jesús

La Ribera

Café de la Ribera
Casa Delfin
Mundial Bar
Al Passatore
Rodrigo
Tèxtil Cafè
Txirimiri

Raval

Bar Kasparo
Granja M Viader
Mesón David

Gràcia

Flash Flash
Virreina Bar

Ports & Shoreline

Agua
El Rebujito de Moncho's
Salamanca
La Miranda del Museu
Xiringuitó Escribà

Poble Sec & Sants

Bar Primavera
Fundació Joan Miró

Barri Gòtic

Barri Gòtic

Restaurants

Agut

C/Gignàs 16, 08002 (93 315 17 09). Metro Jaume I.
Meals served 1.30-4pm, 9pm-midnight Tue-Sat; 1.30-
4pm Sun. Closed Aug. **Average** €€. **Credit** MC, V.
A staid meeting place for well-heeled Catalans of a
certain age, Agut is known for its fresh pasta and huge,
tender steaks. Fish dishes can also be excellent. The
menu changes seasonally and food is imaginatively
presented. Even the set lunch (€9) is prefaced with
amuse-bouches. The pudding list also throws up a few
surprises, not least a glorious mascarpone ice-cream in
a lemon and ginger 'soup'.

Amaya

La Rambla 20-24, 08002 (93 302 61 38/
www.amaya.com-actiu.es). Metro Drassanes. **Meals
served** 1-5.30pm, 8.30pm-midnight daily. **Average** €€.
Credit AmEx, DC, MC, V.
Enter through the bar, and the deeper you go, the smarter
it gets; the fruit machines and black tobacco of the
entrance segue into a womblike haven of peach tones and
table linen a couple of rooms in. Formerly the domain of
actors, writers, opera singers and politicians, Amaya is
now a respected lunch venue for office workers and the
odd tourist. The menu comprises mainly Basque
specialities, with plenty of merluza (hake) and bacalao
(cod); try them a la Santure with garlic and vinegar or
al pil pil with garlic and chillies.

Ample 24

C/Ample 24, 08002 (93 319 19 27). Metro Barceloneta or
Drassanes. **Meals served** 1-4.30pm Mon; 1-4.30pm, 8.30-
11.30pm Tue-Sun. **Average** €. **Credit** AmEx, DC, MC, V.
A quietly stylish little hideaway with stone walls,
watercolours and muted jazz. During the day there is no
à la carte – just a fixed price menu that, at €8, must be
one of the best deals around. The starters include great
soups and dishes such as tostada de revoltillo (roughly,
scrambled egg on toast) bursting with chunks of
botifarra, asparagus, shrimps and garlic, followed by
simpler main courses: grilled salmon marinated in
orange, honey and soy sauce or rabbit stew. Desserts are
not quite as creative, but nor are they really needed after
such huge portions.

Ateneu Gastronomic

Plaça de Sant Miquel 2 bis, 08002 (93 302 11 98). Metro
Jaume I or Liceu. **Meals served** 1-3.30pm, 8.15-11.30pm
Mon-Fri; 8.15-11.30pm Sat. Closed 3wks Aug. **Average**
€€. **Credit** AmEx, DC, MC, V.

Say cheese

Drive along the highways and byways of Spain and the only cows you're likely to see are the huge black silhouetted bulls perched on hilltops advertising sherry. No – Galicia apart, Spain's often largely parched and mountainous landscape is no place for frolicking Friesians, a fact reflected not only in the hens'-teeth nature of fresh milk but also in the variety of sheep's and goat's cheeses.

There are over 100 types of Spanish cheese, most made by hand. Manchego is, of course, the best known: a hard, dense cheese made with sheep's milk from La Mancha and endlessly promoted at home and internationally, to the detriment of other lesser-known and perhaps more interesting types. Other widely available denominación de origen cheeses include firm, nutty roncal, a sheep's cheese from Navarra; idiazábal, a strong, almost spicy Basque sheep's cheese; and cabrales,

a superb blue cheese from Asturias, which is made from a mixture of sheep's, goat's and cow's milk and aged for three months in limestone caves.

Others to look out for include zamorano, a hard sheep's cheese made with unpasteurised milk, and cebreiro, also made with unpasteurised milk, this time from Galician cows, and with a distinctive shape, like a sinking soufflé. Catalonia, too, has a couple of excellent local cheeses; garrotxa is a smooth goat's cheese with a walnutty flavour, and the hugely popular mató is a soft, fresh cheese, very similar to ricotta and generally served drizzled with honey as a dessert. Over in the Balearics, meanwhile, Minorca produces mahón, a cow's milk cheese that can be eaten fresh but is even better after maturing in oil for three months or so.

For an interesting selection of lesser-known cheeses, try the Formatgeria La Seu, just

Dig into the menu of this 'gastronomic club', run with tremendous enthusiasm by gourmet and bibliophile Ernest Nuñez, and you will occasionally strike gold. The sopa de pescador is not the city's finest fish soup, but a starter of asparagus with bittersweet passion fruit reduction works well. The dishes change on a regular basis, but if the rack of lamb appears, make sure you order it. The merluza (hake) with creamed black olives and onion confit can be fantastic (when it hasn't been kept waiting around on a hotplate). And the puddings at Ateneu Gastronomic touch the soul. For example, smokers will love the moscatell sorbet infused with Montecristo No.4. Oenophiles are treated to a 620-strong wine list.

off the Plaça Sant Jaume in the Barri Gòtic. It is situated in the city's first butter-making factory and run by a friendly and helpful Scot, Katherine McLaughlin. There are tastings (three cheeses accompanied by a glass of wine for €1.50) every day, and Katherine runs cheesemaking and tasting courses once a month.

Formatgeria La Seu

C/Dagueria 16, 08002 (93 412 65 48). Metro Jaume I. **Open** 10am-2pm, 5-8pm Tue-Sat. **No credit cards**.

Café de l'Acadèmia ★

C/Lledó 1, 08002 (93 319 82 53/93 315 00 26). Metro Jaume I. **Meals served** 9am-noon, 1.30-4pm, 8.45-11.30pm Mon-Fri. Closed 2wks Aug. **Average** €€. **Credit** AmEx, MC, V.

On everybody's list of favourite Barcelona restaurants, the Acadèmia is still turning out superb modern Catalan dishes at reasonable prices. Highlights include pintado rostit (roast guinea fowl) with a tiny tarte tatin and risotto with duck foie gras and grapes. At lunchtime the stone-walled dining room and wonderful terrace on the medieval Plaça Sant Just throng with politicians from the nearby Generalitat. At night the restaurant plays host to everyone else. Book ahead.

Polenta. *See p36.*

Can Culleretes ★

C/Quintana 5, 08002 (93 317 30 22). Metro Liceu.
Meals served 1.30-4pm, 9-11pm Tue-Sat; 1.30-4pm Sun.
Closed 3wks July. **Average** €. **Credit** MC, V.
Founded in 1786, and allegedly the second oldest
restaurant in Spain (the oldest being Botín in Madrid),
Can Culleretes is still filling its warren of dining rooms
with merry punters. Traditional dishes like roast lechón
(suckling pig), cuixa d'oca amb pomes (goose leg with
apples) and a three-course menu of daisy-fresh seafood
are served up with friendly efficiency. Prices are
unbeatable, particularly for wine; unfortunately, all
Barcelona is aware of this, so you may need to book.

Los Caracoles

C/Escudellers 14, 08002 (93 302 31 85). Metro Liceu.
Meals served 1pm-midnight daily. **Average** €€€.
Credit AmEx, DC, MC, V.
Jostle your way through the sweating chefs slaving away
in their Dantean galley, check in with the Bond-villain
maître d', then retire to the bar and watch how they
immolate the crema catalana until your name is called.
The food is wildly variable; the same meal might include
undercooked arròs negre sloshing in too much liquid; a
doleful sole, tasting a little tired, accompanied by tinned,
yes, tinned carrots; excellent grilled squid and superb

LOMBARDO
Restaurants

Five minutes from Plaza Catalunya on Barcelona's top shopping boulevard. Relaxed atmosphere and delicious modern Catalan cuisine. Summer terrace.

Rambla Catalunya, 49 - 51
Tel. 93 487 48 42

Just off the Ramblas by the Plaça del Pi. Lively tapas restaurant with open kitchen and exceptional seafood. Outside terrace.

Pl. Sant Josep Oriol, 9 (Pl. del Pi)
Tel. 93 302 62 43

Next to Barcelona football stadium. Beautiful restaurant with groundbreaking design. Eclectic Mediterranean cuisine and a relaxing garden.

Travessera de les Corts, 64 - 68
Tel. 93 448 35 52

navajas (razor clams). The place is labyrinthine and oozes character from every cranny, but at worst it can become an overpriced tourist canteen.

Cervantes

C/Cervantes 7, 08002 (93 317 33 84). Metro Jaume I.
Meals served *Bar* 7am-8pm Mon-Fri. *Restaurant* noon-4pm Mon-Fri. Closed Aug. **Average** €. **Credit** AmEx, DC, MC, V.

A set menu (€8) of sturdy Catalan fare might involve a lentil dish or habitas con jamón (baby broad beans with ham) to start, followed by a casserole or grilled meat, at this bustling, friendly lunch-only restaurant. Small tables and plenty of them can make your neighbours' elbows a frustrating feature of the meal.

Cometacinc

C/Cometa 5, 08002 (93 310 15 58). Metro Jaume I.
Meals served 8pm-midnight Mon, Wed-Sun. **Average** €€. **Credit** MC, V.

A cathedral-sized doorway leads into a surprisingly cosy space with burnished wood furnishings, and a peculiar line in whale song and sounds-of-the-rainforest relaxation music. The food is adventurous Mediterranean that's done a bit of backpacking in Asia with a brief stop-off at a chefs' seminar on tower presentation. Try the tottering stack of fried yucca chips mortared with guacamole and chicken, the excellent house salad, the impossibly creamy goat's cheese cannelloni with caramelised onion, or the seared tuna with sesame and apricot confit. Desserts are good but some of the wines are rather heftily marked up.

El Gran Café

C/Avinyó 9, 08002 (93 318 79 86). Metro Liceu. **Meals served** 1-4.30pm, 8pm-12.30am Mon-Sat. **Average** €€. **Credit** AmEx, DC, MC, V.

Everything in this fading but still elegant brasserie is geared towards making the foreigner happy. Bread comes with butter; waiters come with aprons; dinner comes with a pianist, and rather touchingly, vegetables come with salad. Ignore the bids for the tourist dollar on the menu (roast beef), and head for the wafer-thin carpaccios or the magret de pato (duck), both of which are delicious. Old-fashioned service and levels of comfort conspire to make this the sort of place your mother would love.

Hostal El Pintor

C/Sant Honorat 7, 08002 (93 301 40 65). Metro Jaume I.
Meals served 1.30-4.30pm, 8pm-midnight daily.
Average €€€. **Credit** AmEx, DC, MC, V.

The most central of the Travi restaurants (*see also p205* **Can Travi Nou**) occupies a carefully restored 19th-century artists' studio, with a grandfather clock, checked

Elegant, bustling **Les Quinze Nits** *p39* has branches at **La Crema Canela** Passatge Madoz 6, 08002, Barri Gòtic (93 318 2744); **La Dolça Herminia** C/Magdalenes 27, 08002, Barri Gòtic (93 317 0676); **La Fonda** C/Escudellers 10, Barri Gòtic 08002 (93 301 7515).

Els Quatre Gats. *See p39.*

tablecloths and wooden beams. Brick walls heave with strings of dried peppers, plates, paintings and other artisan paraphernalia. A range of competently cooked Catalan classics is on offer, including snails, stuffed aubergines, charcoal-grilled cod with roasted peppers, sea bream baked in salt, or pigs' trotters. Prices are perhaps a little inflated but this doesn't put off the many locals who eat here. The lunch menú offers much better value at €16.20.

Mastroqué

C/Codols 29, 08002 (93 301 79 42). Metro Drassanes or Jaume I. **Meals served** 9-11.30pm Mon; 1.30-3.30pm, 9-11.30pm Tue-Fri; 9-11.30pm Sat. Closed most of Aug. **Average** €€. **Credit** MC, V.

Burnt yellow walls and mellow lighting give this unexpectedly spacious restaurant an intimate feel. Mastroqué offers a small but interesting selection of regional dishes from France and Spain, served as media raciones (in other words, you can have two). Duck in all its forms is the speciality, but unusual dishes such as morcilla con mermelada de cebolla (black pudding with onion marmalade) also feature. At lunchtime there is only a set menu with limited options, but all are well chosen.

Mercè Vins

C/Amargós 1, 08002 (93 302 60 56). Metro Urquinaona. **Meals served** 8am-5pm Mon-Thur; 8am-5pm, 9pm-midnight Fri; 8am-noon Sat. **Average** €. **Credit** V.

A cosy place tucked into a sidestreet above the cathedral, with yellow walls, fresh flowers and fabulously friendly staff. In the morning this is a popular place for breakfasts and bocadillos, at lunchtime there is a set menu only (€7.40). This features a better choice than normal, with interesting Catalan dishes such as trinxat de la Cerdanya (think bubble and squeak with bacon) to start, followed by gall dindi (turkey) with roquefort sauce or llom (pork) with almonds and prunes. On Friday nights, pa amb tomàquet (*see p59*) is served with ham and cheese.

Mesón Jesús

C/Cecs de la Boqueria 4, 08002 (93 317 46 98). Metro Liceu. **Meals served** 1-4pm, 8-11pm Mon-Fri. Closed Aug-early Sept. **Average** €. **Credit** MC, V.

Gingham tablecloths, oak barrels, beaming waiters and traditional Spanish cooking make for a satisfyingly authentic experience in the heart of the labyrinthine Gothic quarter. The choice is limited, but dishes are reliably good and inexpensive to boot. Try the sautéed green beans with ham to start, followed by superb grilled prawns or a tasty zarzuela (fish stew). Tourists are looked after with multilingual menus, but there's no shortage of lunching locals during the day, drawn in by

Just off the Plaça Reial, **Herboristeria del Rei** (C/Vidre 1) is a sumptuously ornate herb shop, its walls lined with tiny specimen drawers.

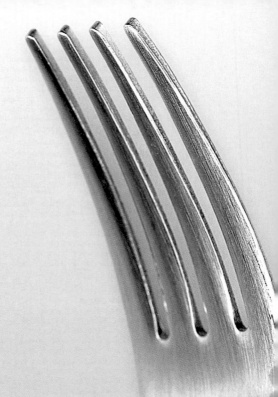

taxidermista...cafè restaurant
Plaça Reial 8   08002 Barcelona   tel. 93 412 45 36

a good-value set menu containing the odd surprise such as tasty courgettes stuffed with pork and tomato. This is also a child-friendly place, where half portions will be served on request.

Món Obert

Passatge Escudellers 5, 08002 (93 301 72 73). Metro Liceu. **Meals served** 1-4pm Mon-Wed; 1-4pm, 9pm-midnight Thur-Sat. **Average** €. **Credit** AmEx, DC, MC, V.

The spacious airy ambience of this modest restaurant doubles as an informal cultural centre, with a mini-library, gift shop and rotating art exhibitions converging to justify the holistically inspired name (literally, open world). The varied set menu includes meat, fish and pastas as well as options clearly pegged for vegetarians (umpteen lentil variations), with the flavours of five continents freely sharing the same plate. Excess dicing and a liberal use of ginger and fruity condiments give a chutney-like dimension to much of the cooking, though the lunch menu is cheap enough and the service warm and attentive.

Oolong

C/Gignás 25, 08002 (93 315 12 59). Metro Jaume I. **Meals served** 8pm-midnight Mon-Sat; 8pm-11am Sun. **Average** €. **No credit cards**.

The best noisy birthdays

Agua
See p175.

Flash Flash
See p170.

Fuse
See p132.

Meson David
See p78.

Oven
See p208.

Shalimar
See p82.

Taverna Can Margarit
See p199.

El Salón. *See p39.*

The one problem with Oolong is its immense popularity with the global hipsters roaming the Gothic quarter. In the height of the summer, it can be extremely difficult to get a table and you may feel rushed once you're there. The food is innovative and vaguely oriental in flavour, with wonderfully aromatic, Middle Eastern-style salads (oranges with caramelised almonds and a rose petal vinaigrette, anyone?) and delicious chicken dishes, but the funky music and beautiful people propping up the bar are really what the place is all about.

Pla ★

C/Bellafila 5, 08002 (93 412 65 52). Metro Jaume I.
Meals served 9pm-midnight Mon-Thur, Sun; 9pm-1am Fri, Sat. **Average** €€. **Credit** MC, V.
A dramatic, split-level space painted in deep colours and featuring uplit modern artworks and low lighting. The menu at Pla is a modish mix of Mediterranean and oriental dishes; Thai fish curry is well executed, as is the duck confit with grapes or the chicken pancake. Salads and carpaccios can also be fantastic here, and puddings round things off with panache. Try, for example, the own-made lemon ice-cream, dotted with fresh raspberries and lethally doused in vodka, or the pear tatin served with a hot chocolate sauce.

Polenta

C/Ample 51, 08002 (93 268 14 29). Metro Jaume I.
Meals served 1pm-midnight Mon-Thur, Sun; 1pm-1am Fri, Sat. **Average** €. **Credit** AmEx, MC, V.
An unusual concept for Barcelona, Polenta specialises in an unlikely, but appealing, fusion of Mediterranean and Japanese influences. Dishes tend to be on the light and healthy side. Yakitori chicken and leek sticks, or leafy salad with tofu and dabs of salty pink polenta, are served (throughout the day) to a suitably international, suitably modern soundtrack. For pudding, try the optimistically named Aphrodisiac, comprising ice-cream, chocolate and candied ginger.

La Poste

Vins i Caves La Catedral (Plaça Ramon Berenguer el Gran 1) is a friendly little shop with excellent wines and cavas from all over Spain.

C/Gignàs 23, 08002 (93 315 15 04). Metro Jaume I.
Meals served 1-4.30pm, 8-11.30pm Mon-Fri; 1-4.30pm Sat, Sun. Closed late Aug-early Sept. **Average** €. **Credit** MC, V.
Home to what has to be the best-value lunch menu in Barcelona with enormous portions of hearty, no-nonsense staples, La Poste attracts a diverse and loyal crowd, from postal workers from the nearby Correus to Catalan ladies who lunch. The dining area is oddly sterile in atmosphere and enjoys more air-conditioning than is called for, but no one's complaining when faced with an entire tortilla as a starter.

Taxidermista. See p40.

Pou Dols

C/Baixada de Sant Miquel 6, 08002 (93 412 05 79).
Metro Jaume I or Liceu. **Meals served** 1.30-4pm,
9-11.30pm Tue-Sat. Closed 3wks Aug. **Average** €€€.
Credit AmEx, DC, MC, V.
Brief, intense flavours, unusual combinations, elaborate
presentation: in less assured hands this could all
crumble into tiresome pretension. Pou Dols, however,
offers excellent food, friendly service and an eclectic
wine list (at a price). Crab and asparagus cannelloni
drizzled with mango sauce are delicate parcels of
delight, or try seared sea bream with tiny squid, baby
broad beans and a rich meat jus. Desserts are sublime:
a coulant breaks to reveal its dark, molten centre, and
peppery aubergine purée served with lime sorbet is as
delicious as it is unusual.

Els Quatre
Gats *(right)* is
an attractive
place for a
cofee and
some good,
though pricey,
tapas. Built
by Puig i
Cadafalch, it
was for many
years the
meeting point
of bohemian
Barcelona.
Major artists
of the day,
such as
Rusiñol and
Casas,
painted
pictures for it
and the menu
cover was
Picasso's first
paid
commission.

Els Quatre Gats

*C/Montsió 3 bis, 08002 (93 302 42 40). Metro
Urquinaona.* **Meals served** 1pm-1am Mon-Sat;
5pm-1am Sun. Closed 3wks Aug. **Average** €€€.
Credit AmEx, DC, MC, V.

Charming Modernista architecture combined with its
history as an artists' meeting place make Quatre Gats an
'experience', though one that has been sorely
compromised by its own success. Serving traditional
Catalan cuisine, the 'Four Cats' is nowadays overfull,
overrated and overpriced. The food is competent but not
outstanding, the waiters supercilious, and the tables
crammed so close it is only the easy-listening classics of
the pianist and violinist (playing on the four catguts,
presumably) that allow privacy. If you must come (and
you probably must) a less adventurous lunch-time menu
offers the same experience for a fraction of the price –
without the violinist.

Les Quinze Nits

Plaça Reial 6, 08002 (93 317 30 75). Metro Liceu.
Meals served 1-3.45pm, 8.30-11.30pm daily. **Average** €.
Credit AmEx, DC, MC, V.

Opinions are sharply divided on this innovative chain of
elegant, bustling restaurants, but to cavil at the
occasionally variable quality of the main courses (and we
would urge you to avoid the paella, or any other dish
likely to have been prepared in industrial quantities) is
to overlook the rock-bottom prices, incongruous in such
a setting. Few other places can offer sophisticated menus
of modern Catalan dishes in this price range, as the
queues testify. For a shorter wait, head to one of the many
branches around the city.

El Salón ★

*C/Hostal d'en Sol 6-8, 08002 (93 315 21 59). Metro
Jaume I.* **Meals served** 2-5pm, 8.30pm-midnight
Mon-Sat. Closed 2 wks Aug. **Average** €€. **Credit**
AmEx, MC, V.

The cuisine at El Salón defies all attempts at labelling.
Starters include such combinations as mushroom
carpaccio with figs, or lentils with squid and raita. Mains
feature the likes of roast rabbit in a creamy saffron sauce,
or satay lamb and chicken with coconut rice. All the dishes
are rich and good. The restaurant is a relaxed and informal
place, with baroque touches giving the mismatched
furniture and high-ceilinged room a bohemian air. There
is also a handful of outdoor tables to be had.

Slokai

C/Palau 5, 08002 (93 317 90 94). Metro Jaume I.
Meals served 1.30-4pm, 9pm-midnight Mon-Fri;
9pm-midnight Sat. **Average** €€. **Credit** MC, V.

Shunka. *See p43.*

A white and airy space dotted with colourful artworks and cheerfully run by a team of Latin American waiters. The menu at Slokai includes somewhat self-consciously trendy ingredients such as kangaroo and ostrich, and plenty of fusion menu stalwarts (for example, chicken brochette with sesame and soy sauce or grilled duck liver with mango sauce), some prepared more confidently than others. There are also a few safer bets in the form of Italian classics – spinach tortellini smothered with tomato and parmesan, basil gnocchi and so on. The set lunch menu is good value with a self-service buffet of interesting salads to start, followed by risotto, pasta or a meat dish.

Taxidermista
Plaça Reial 8, 08002 (93 412 45 36). Metro Liceu. **Meals served** 1.30-4pm, 8.30pm-12.30am Tue-Sun. **Average** €€. **Credit** DC, MC, V.
As its name implies, this was once a shop full of stuffed animals, and before that a natural history museum, but Taxidermista's owners have resisted the lure of stags' heads and turned it into an elegant square restaurant where shafts of sunlight fall on to a black and white tiled floor. The menu features high-quality dishes with a French influence, such as rèmol (turbot) with cider sauce and apple purée, or poularde stuffed with espinacas a la catalana and served with leek crisps. Outside there is an ample terrace under an arcade of the Plaça Reial, where tapas are served all day.

International

Machiroku

C/Moles 21, 08002 (93 412 60 82). Metro Urquinaona.
Meals served 1.30-3.30pm, 8.30-11.30pm Mon-Fri;
8.30-11.30pm Sat. Closed 2wks Aug. **Average** €.
No credit cards.

A few steps from the culinary wasteland of Plaça
Catalunya, Machiroku provides an oasis of Japanese
calm. Service is charming and friendly and the three
different lunchtime menus offer incredibly good value for
money. These might include a seaweed and sesame salad,
miso soup and generous portions of sushi, sashimi or
nigiri zushi, although there are plenty of other dishes to
choose from if you go à la carte.

Il Mercante di Venezia

*C/Josep Anselm Clavé 11, 08002 (93 317 18 28). Metro
Drassanes.* **Meals served** 1.30-3.45pm, 8.30-11.45pm
Tue-Sun. **Average** €. **Credit** DC, MC, V.

A grand baroque entrance with ornate stencilling, heavy
damask drapes scooped in with tasselled cords, and
tumbling bowls of fruit leads into a dark cave of a
restaurant, whose chiaroscuro intimacy is a hair's
breadth from being suffocating. Salads are disappointing
– pomodoro i arugula comes balanced on a hillock of
unrequested iceberg and carrot – and pasta dishes look

Not for those
with delicate
noses, the
**Casa del
Bacalao**
(C/Comtal 8)
sells nothing
but salt cod.
Soak it
overnight in
three changes
of water and
you'd never
know it
wasn't fresh.

more convincingly Italian on the page than on the plate, but the pizzas are good, with a wide variety that includes several wholemeal options. The nearby branch, Le Tre Venezie, offers a similiar menu in airier surroundings.

El Paraguayo

C/Parc 1, 08002 (93 302 14 41). Metro Drassanes.
Meals served 1-4pm, 8pm-midnight Tue-Thur, Sun; 1-4pm, 8pm-1am Fri, Sat. **Average** €€€. **Credit** AmEx, DC, MC, V.

El Paraguayo is carnivore heaven – chunks of beef, blackened on the outside and oozing red at the centre – are served on wooden boards, with only a bowl of garlicky chimichurri sauce as a token nod to plant life. It's delicious, but no place to bring a vegetarian or anyone who cried during *Bambi*. Side dishes include a selection of salads, corn on the cob and yucca chips. If you have any room left, pancakes filled with dulce de leche (caramelised condensed milk) will finish you off. The warm, pine interior is covered in South American art, and service is friendly and informal. Did we mention the meat?

Peimong

C/Templers 6-10, 08002 (93 318 28 73). Metro Jaume I.
Meals served 1-4.30pm, 8-11.30pm Tue-Sun. **Average** €. **Credit** MC, V.

Not, perhaps, the fanciest-looking restaurant around (think Peruvian gimcracks and strip lighting) or indeed the fanciest-looking food, but it sure tastes like the real thing. Try the ceviche for an explosion of lime and coriander or the spicy corn tamales. Service is particularly warm and friendly, there are two types of Peruvian beer and even – for the very nostalgic or the hypoglycaemic – Inca Kola.

Shunka

C/Sagristans 5, 08002 (93 412 49 91). Metro Jaume I.
Meals served 1.30-3.30pm, 8.30-11.30pm Tue-Fri; 2-4pm, 8.30-11.30pm Sat, Sun. **Average** €. **Credit** AmEx, DC, MC, V.

The great-value menú del dia (€11.80) in this excellent Japanese restaurant might include miso soup, salmon salad, prawn and vegetable tempura, mixed sushi and a drink. A small, well-chosen menu includes main courses ranging from sushi and sashimi to substantial rice and noodle dishes – udon con fritura de langostina y verduras mezclas (prawn and vegetable tempura in soup) stands out. Desserts include creamy green tea ice-cream and saké truffles. Superchef Ferran Adrià occasionally drops in here for lunch, eating at the bar overlooking the kitchen – a good choice as other tables are poorly lit.

La Verònica. *See p45.*

Tokyo

C/Comtal 20, 08002 (93 317 61 80). Metro Urquinaona.
Meals served 1.30-4pm, 8-11pm Mon-Sat. Closed Aug.
Average €€. **Credit** AmEx, DC, MC, V.

Tokyo is one of the best of the tsunami of Japanese restaurants to hit Barcelona. Its easily missed entrance leads to a quiet, peaceful space: stone-clad walls give it a cave-like feel, and wooden screens positioned between the tables keep things intimate. The fixed lunch menú (€15) is not automatically offered but worth requesting if you want to keep prices down; it includes udon noodle soup, a great seafood salad, sushi and, best of all, the sukiyaki of paper-thin meat and vegetables cooked at your table.

La Verònica

C/Avinyó 25, 08002 (93 412 11 22). Metro Liceu.
Meals served 7.30pm-1.30am Tue-Fri; 1pm-1.30am Sat, Sun. Closed 2wks Feb, 2wks Aug. **Average** €.
Credit MC, V.

A colourful, elegantly constructed space with food to match: thin, crispy pizzas and designer salads. In the summer, tourists fill the outside tables on Plaça George Orwell, but late nights and winter months draw a fashionably clad, mainly gay, local crowd, to munch on such delights as carrot and parsnip shavings doused in ginger vinaigrette.

Vegetarian

Govinda

Plaça Vila de Madrid 4-5, 08002 (93 318 77 29).
Metro Liceu. **Meals served** 1-4pm Mon, Sun;
1-4pm, 8-11pm Tue-Thur; 1-4pm, 8-11.45pm Fri, Sat.
Closed 2wks Aug. **Average** €. **Credit** AmEx, DC,
MC, V.

Govinda's good-value lunch menú (€8) attracts all types of diners from suits to students, with three courses that include a basic salad buffet, spicy soups and creative main dishes – such as pumpkin patties with walnuts and tomato jam – finishing off with coconut pudding, say, or rose petal ice-cream. The à la carte menu is substantially more expensive, although the thalis are a good way to sample a wide range of specialities such as raita, kofta, chapatis, sabji, chutneys and dhal. Drinks include fresh juices, lassis, teas and coffee but no alcohol, and smoking is not permitted in the main room during the day.

Juicy Jones

*C/Cardenal Casañas 7, 08002 (606 204 906). Metro
Liceu.* **Meals served** 1.30-11.30pm daily. **Average** €.
No credit cards.

Colmado Afro-Latino (Via Laietana 15) has a fantastic range of liquor and foodstuffs from Africa and Latin America, including Argentine maté, Brazilian cachaça and palm wine from Cameroon.

The maverick veggie option with hallucinogenic graffiti (the look is updated every year or so), thumping eurotrance and young scatty waitresses fresh off their Erasmus schemes. The soup, served with wholewheat breads, changes daily, and there is a thali plate of roast vegetables, sauces, cereals and pulses. Portions are substantial and carefully presented and, as the name suggests, this place specialises in freshly squeezed juices, fruity shakes and yoghurt smoothies. Smoking is not allowed.

Cafés & Bars

L'Antiquari
C/Veguer 13, 08002 (93 310 04 35). Metro Jaume I.
Open *mid Sept-May* 5pm-2am daily. *June-mid Sept* 10am-2.30am daily. **No credit cards**.
Dark wooden fittings, an old joanna in the corner, nostalgic '80s electronica on the stereo along with 12-bar blues anthems; staff here know what they like, and if the rest of the world has moved on, well, that's just too bad. The outside tables in the stunning Plaça del Rei allow for more contemplative drinking.

Arc Café
C/Carabassa 19, 08002 (93 302 52 04). Metro Jaume I.
Open 10am-2am Mon-Thur; 10am-3am Fri, Sat; 10am-2am Sun. **Credit** AmEx, DC, MC, V.
A welcoming café that has become a nerve centre for the locals' campaign to save the historic street from development. There's food available throughout the day, from good breakfasts (including muesli, yoghurt and honey) to more substantial dishes such as arroz con gambas or cordero con pure de patatas. The high-ceilinged main room has a great selection of magazines, or there's a tiny room upstairs.

L'Ascensor
C/Bellafila 3, 08002 (93 318 53 47). Metro Jaume I.
Open 6.30pm-3am daily. **No credit cards**.
Enter through the eponymous mahogany lift with its original sliding doors and bevelled glass, into this low-ceilinged den. The gently quaint decor (gilt lamps, marble tables with wicker chairs, and lots of dark wood) is redolent of fin-de-siècle Paris, but the loud funky sounds and the fortifying Mojito and Caipirinha cocktails drag it, rather confused, into the 21st century.

The Bagel Shop
C/Canuda 25, 08002 (93 302 41 61). Metro Catalunya.
Open 9.30am-9.30pm Mon-Sat; 11am-4pm Sun. **No credit cards**.

The queue outside the **Forn de Pa Sant Jordi** (C/Llibreteria 8) is testimony to the delights inside. A good place to try seasonal cakes such as marzipan panellets at Hallowe'en.

Govinda. See p45.

Riding the new wave

Take an awkward space and prepare according to Love Your Ventilation Duct School of Design; add a couple of young and good-looking chefs with their names emblazoned on their chests and preferably visible through glass; stir in a 'concepto degustación' menu; a pinch of wit; a sprinkling of irony; infuse the whole thing with science, and you are on the way to creating a New Wave Catalan Restaurant. The only thing that remains is the purchase of a dozen carbon dioxide canisters in order to create dishes entirely from foam and some teapots from which to serve soup. Other rules dictate that ice-cream must be made with savoury ingredients (thyme, say, or romesco sauce) and another that says that puddings must be broken down into their component parts, layered and served in a shotglass.

Location is also important. The Born area is a fertile ground for this type of restaurant; **Santa Maria** (*see p108*) and **Espai Sucre** (*see p102*) are past masters of the art; a newer and immensely successful addition is **Comerç 24** (*pictured, right, and see p101*); and **Arrel** (*see p97*) is showing promising signs – botifarra sausage where the fat has been replaced with white chocolate, for example. Up in Gràcia the boys at **Ot** (*see p162*) know how to wield a canister, and you will find nods to these trends in most of the top-end restaurants; witness the sachet of chocolate-covered Pop Rocks among the petit fours at **El Racó d'en Freixa** (*see p163*), also in Gràcia, and the deconstructed, foamed crema catalana at **Gaig** (*see p206*) in Horta.

The granddaddy of them all, the man that launched a thousand siphons, is Ferran Adrià (*below*) whose fantastical, playful creations fuse science with poetry. An aubergine ravioli is served with a yoghurt foam and flavoured with a melted Fisherman's Friend; 'Kellogg's paella' involves featherlight, toasted grains of rice infused with

shellfish and served in a plastic sachet, to be ripped open and the contents poured into the mouth; and exploding ravioli, where the pasta is a gossamer-thin sheet of squid, filled with coconut milk, which bursts in the mouth. Tortilla is served as three mounds of foam: one potato, one egg and one onion. Even British food is given a twist, with a paper cone full of tiny battered fish, and an exuberant take on the ice-cream wafer sandwich; here, the wafers are crunchy and cheese-flavoured and the ice-cream is parmesan.

Adrià has finally been recognised as one of the world's finest cooks – with three Michelin stars – and almost certainly the world's most inventive. Gourmet pilgrims travel from around the world to the remote culinary mecca of El Bulli, several

kilometres from Roses, up an almost inaccessible dirt track. It is rumoured that only a third of the kitchen staff is paid, and still there are chefs lining up to work with him.

Some of the most coveted positions are in Adrià's Barri Gòtic workshop, where he spends half the year (when the restaurant is closed) creating fantasies in foam and leafing through his library, looking for dishes to reinvent. He and his team of alchemists play around with texture, temperature and smell, creating aerosols evoking the mustiness of a forest, or the salty air and seaweed of the coast.

Should you not have the patience to endure the year-long waiting list at El Bulli, there is a solution. In spring 2002, Adrià commissioned a set of aerosols for domestic use: taronger en flor (orange blossom), mar (sea) and bosc humit (damp woodland). Simply spray over the table, allow the aromas to settle, and revel in the gasps of wonder from your delighted dinner guests.

El Bulli
Cala Montjoi (972 15 04 57/www.elbulli.com). By car A7 or N11 north (7km/4.5 miles from Roses)/by train RENFE from Sants or Passeig de Gràcia to Figueres, then bus to Roses, then taxi. **Meals served** *Apr-June 8-10pm Wed-Sun. June-Sept 8-10pm daily. Closed Oct-Mar.* **Average** *€€€€.* **Credit** *AmEx, DC, MC, V.*

Foreigners flock to this bright yellow and fairly cramped café for a variety of bagels – plain, poppyseed, onion – combined with every conceivable topping; try sobrasada (spicy Mallorcan sausage) with cream cheese. The Bagel Shop's Canadian owner indulges his homeland's breakfast tradition to the hilt with two very filling pancakes with maple syrup, while on Sunday there's egg 'n' bacon with toasted bagel for scores of homesick Brits.

Bar Celta

C/Mercè 16, 08002 (93 315 00 06). Metro Drassanes. **Open** noon-midnight Mon-Sat. **Credit** MC, V.
This tapas bar is not pretty with its bright lights and outdated '60s decor, but it is friendly and fun. Huge trays laden predominantly with seafood tapas line the bar, where patrons wade ankle-deep in screwed-up napkins. Particularly good are the rabas (deep-fried chunks of squid) and pimientos del padron (small, mostly mild, green peppers).

Bar del Pi

Plaça Sant Josep Oriol 1, 08002 (93 302 21 23). Metro Liceu. **Open** 9am-11pm Mon, Wed-Sun. **Credit** MC, V.
The tables outside this bustling and much-loved bar offer front-row seats for viewing buskers, tourists and the weekend art market against the majestic backdrop of the Santa Maria del Pi church. Inside, space is cramped. An old piano at the back helps foster the friendly atmosphere.

Bilbao-Berria

Plaça Nova 3, 08002 (93 317 0124). Metro Jaume I. **Open** 9am-midnight daily. **Credit** AmEx, MC, V.
Bilbao-Berria is a useful meeting point in the cathedral square. Choose from the dozens of fresh and colourful pintxos lining the counter, or order a cazuelito – a small earthenware dish – of one of the delicacies (usually seafood) on display at the end of the bar. There are plenty of tables in the shade outside and an excellent restaurant downstairs.

Bliss

Plaça Sant Just 4, 08002 (93 268 10 22). Metro Jaume I. **Open** 10am-11.30pm Mon-Fri; 1.30pm-midnight Sat. **Credit** MC, V.
Bliss offers a tempting selection of own-made brownies and cakes (including lemon, ginger and walnut), quiches and fresh fruit juice. You can enjoy them in a relaxing sunken sitting-room area with zebra print sofas and international magazines or, in spring and summer, outside in the quiet medieval square. The staff can be less than friendly on occasions.

Juicy Jones. *See p45.*

El Bosc de les Fades

*Passatge de la Banca, 08002 (93 317 26 49). Metro
Drassanes.* **Open** 10.30am-1am Mon-Thur; 10.30am-2am
Fri, Sat; 10.30am-1am Sun. **No credit cards**.

The 'fairies' forest' requires a very particular mood. As
you grope in the semi-darkness you might chance upon
a pointy-eared fairy (an escapee from the nearby wax
museum) kneeling in silent prayer at a waterfall. Or
perhaps you'd care to sip your drinks in the castle
kitchen, complete with inglenook and hanging cauldron.
A very surreal drinking experience.

Buenas Migas

*C/Baixada de Santa Clara 2, off Plaça del Rei, 08002 (93
412 16 86/93 318 37 08). Metro Jaume I.* **Open** 11am-
9pm daily. **Credit** AmEx, MC, V.

Space is limited in this homey café, with the only seats
lined up along the windows that overlook the ancient
stone streets behind the cathedral. The speciality is a
light focaccia bread with a variety of toppings, but the
sweet treats (pear and cream cake or apple crumble) are
pretty special too. The similar branch in the Raval has
tables outside.

Check out the pizzas at highly decorative **Il Mercante di Venezia** (*p41*) and its airier branch **Le Tre Venezie** Plaça Duc de Medinaceli 4, 08002 (93 342 42 52).

Café La Cereria

C/Baixada de Sant Miquel 3-5, 08002 (93 301 85 10).
Metro Liceu. **Open** 9.30am-10pm Mon-Sat.
No credit cards.
This friendly and fresh café, run as a co-operative, is always crowded, but the waiters – many of them co-owners – do their utmost to cope. Vegetarian relief is supplied in the form of creative and healthy sandwiches, and there are milkshakes, fresh juices, a long list of herbal teas and maté. There are quiet tables outside in the Passatge Crèdit.

Cafè d'Estiu

Museu Frederic Marès, Plaça Sant Iu 5, 08002 (93 310 30 14). Metro Jaume I. **Open** *Apr-Sept* 10am-10pm Tue-Sun. Closed Oct-Mar. **No credit cards**.
One of the loveliest outdoor cafés in Barcelona, set in a Gothic courtyard with a stone fish pond and a number of beautiful old orange trees. On offer is a standard selection of coffee, tea, drinks and some light pastries. Cafè d'Estiu is a wonderfully peaceful place to enjoy a quiet drink, but only in summer, as its Catalan name – literally 'summer café' – indicates.

Arc Café. *See p46*.

Café de l'Opera ★

La Rambla 74, 08002 (93 317 75 85/93 302 41 80).
Metro Liceu. **Open** 8am-2.15am Mon-Thur, Sun; 8am-3am
Fri, Sat. **No credit cards**.

Opened around 1890 as a place for Barcelona's elite to see
and be seen after the opera at the Liceu across the street,
this is now Everyman's café, with locals, a large gay
contingent and foreigners of every stripe. There are
standard tapas, good desserts, a long brandy list and a
decent selection of beers. Two comfortable upstairs salons
(recently refurbished) open in the evening.

Café Royale

C/Nou de Zurbano 3, 08002 (93 412 14 33). Metro
Drassanes or Liceu. **Open** 6pm-2.30am Mon-Thur; 6pm-
3am Fri, Sat; 7pm-2.30am Sun. **No credit cards**.

With its pleasantly scuffed look, mellow orange-velvet
curtains and fathomless sofas, this place looks like a
fabulous '70s *Vogue*-style lounge club. Early in the week
you may find space to relax and listen to the dog-eared
library of bossa nova and Latin jazz shelved behind the
DJ's cabinet. At weekends, however, it's packed to
squeaking point with a high-sheen, high-maintenance
fashion crowd.

Café Zurich

*Plaça Catalunya 1, 08002 (93 317 91 53). Metro
Catalunya.* **Open** *June-end Oct* 8am-1am Mon-Fri;
10am-1am Sat. *End Oct-May* 8am-11pm Mon-Fri,
Sun; 8am-midnight Sat. **No credit cards**.
Generations of Barcelonins and travellers have whiled
away afternoons on this sunny, sprawling terrace,
although the original much-loved bar was torn down in
1997 to make way for the El Triangle shopping centre.
The new Zurich was decorated with generic, old-style
fittings (the stopped clock is the only piece salvaged
from the wreckage), which, unsurprisingly, miss the
mark somewhat. Still, the café has regained its status
as a meeting spot for locals, backpackers and other
urban wanderers.

Casa el Molinero

C/Mercè 13, 08002 (93 310 33 83). Metro Drassanes.
Open 6pm-2am daily. **No credit cards**.
Worlds apart from the slickly designed Catalan bars that
pepper the city, this 'tasca' – traditional tapas bar,
typically brightly lit, with whitewashed walls and rustic
decor – along with all the others on this street, presents
an unreconstructed, and very Spanish, face. Enjoy chorizo

Bar Celta. *See p51.*

al diablo (spicy sausage set alight in alcohol) washed down with leche de pantera ('panther's milk'), an opaque alcoholic concoction popular among Spanish teenagers.

Fonfone

C/Escudellers 24, 08002 (93 317 14 24/www.fonfone.com).
Metro Drassanes. **Open** 10pm-2.30am Mon-Thur, Sun;
10pm-3am Fri, Sat. **Credit** MC, V.
A deep bar with a dancefloor lit by the multicoloured radioactive glow of Lego-like brick decorations, Fonfone seems to draw a steady throughput of people on their way somewhere else and looking for any uptempo beats, from drum 'n' bass to house, to spark the evening off. Just across the street you can catch some of the same DJs at the new (and still slightly musty) club Technique.

Glaciar

Plaça Reial 3, 08002 (93 302 11 63). Metro Liceu. **Open**
4pm-2.15am Mon-Sat; 8am-2.15am Sun. **No credit cards**.
Inside, the high ceilings and old dark wood provide the sort of ambience that resists the vagaries of fashion, but Glaciar's real selling point (and it sure ain't the loos) is its terrace on the Plaça Reial. Locals and resident foreigners still congregate here in time-honoured fashion, to people-watch and meet friends.

La Granja

C/Banys Nous 4, 08002 (93 302 69 75). Metro Liceu.
Open 9.30am-2pm, 5-9.30pm Mon-Sat; 5.30-9.30pm Sun.
Closed 3wks end Aug-Sept. **No credit cards**.
This antique-filled café is representative of the many changes that the Gothic quarter has undergone over the centuries: the uneven floors and walls change from wood to tile to stone – and there's even a section of Roman wall in the back. Try the mini-suizo if the standard heaped mug of thick, steaming chocolate and cream (an ordinary suizo) is too much.

Jupiter ★

C/Jupí 4, 08002 (93 268 36 50). Metro Jaume I.
Open 7pm-1am Tue-Thur, Sun; 7pm-2am Fri, Sat.
No credit cards.
Soft lighting, welcoming armchairs and sagging sofas arranged around low tables set the ambience in this great little bar, which must be one of the most chilled out places in town to spend an evening. A tempting choice of crêpes, bocadillos, salads and desserts is served by the very friendly staff in the tiny restaurant area at the back.

Leticia ★

C/Còdols 21, 08002 (93 302 00 74). Metro Drassanes.
Open 7pm-3am Mon, Wed-Sun. **Credit** MC, V.

Bar del Pi. *See p51*.

Leticia is effortlessly cool and supremely relaxed, with kitsch-laden walls, comfy chairs and a sofa on which to chat, play chess and chill out to drum 'n' bass, rare soul, flamenco and jazz. Chatty staff mix a mean cocktail and there's an excellent range of salads, bocadillos, cakes and vegetarian dishes.

Al Limón Negro

C/Escudellers Blancs 3, 08002 (649 314 705). Metro Liceu. **Open** 8pm-2am Tue-Thur, Sun; 8pm-3.30am Fri, Sat. **No credit cards**.

Mellow lighting and muddy primary colours attract a relaxed mix of urban wanderers who play cards in the shadows, chilling to laid-back Brazilian beats under the inevitable slide projections. Occasionally, there's a DJ or band to kick up some dust, and veggie food – tacos, falafel, sandwiches and salads – is usually available on the mezzanine level.

Slices of life

International reporters looked on baffled at a recent anti-globalisation demonstration in Valencia, as protesters handed out slices of bread rubbed with ripe tomato and drizzled with olive oil. What coded call to arms was this? The Catalan red and gold flag, Quatre Barres, made vegetal? Or some kind of international soup kitchen, braced, like the Red Cross, to provide succour and sustenance to those fighting the good fight? No, this was pa amb tomàquet, Catalonia's simplest and most emblematic of dishes, used as a reminder that local produce is the best produce, and that even the mighty emperors of fast-food stand no chance in a cultural battle.

In a recent book, Mallorcan resident Tomàs Graves, son of the poet Robert, tries to claw back some of the cultural identity of his island from the sunburnt hordes of Northern Europeans with an entire tome on the subject. The title, Volem pa amb oli, means 'We want bread and oil' and refers to the cry that went up in their banned language from the hunger-striking Mallorcans imprisoned under Franco. This is not the only book on the topic; in 1984 Leopoldo Pomès published a (not entirely serious) work, entitled The Theory and Practice of Bread With Tomato.

The key, apparently, lies in the tomato. It has to be good, and it has to be ripe. Very ripe. Bread, too, can benefit from just the right amount of ageing – a day is about spot on. Pa amb tomàquet is good with anything, but especially ham, cheese or anchovies, and washed down with copious quantities of hearty red wine. A llesqueria is a place which specialises in such delights; llesque means 'slice', and if the bread is toasted, it becomes a 'torrada'. Good llesqueries include **La Vinateria del Call** (see p66) and **Mercè Vins** (see p33) in the Barri Gòtic or **La Tinaja** (see p125) and **Pla de la Garsa** (see p105) in La Ribera. Restaurants that serve excellent llesques along with heartier a la brasa fare include **La Bodegueta** (see p197) and **La Tomaquera** (see p199) in Poble Sec or **La Parra** (see p198) in Sants.

Café Royale. *See p54.*

Malpaso

C/Rauric 20, 08002 (no phone). Metro Liceu. **Open** 8pm-2.30am Mon-Thur, Sun; 8pm-3am Fri, Sat. **No credit cards**.
With its colourful geometry and arty glassed-in installations, Malpaso is very nearly cool, and yet somehow has the earnest feel of the downstairs bar in a savvy youth hostel. Maybe it's the DJ spinning monsters-of-rock classics mixed with the odd '90s dance track, or maybe it's the studenty noticeboard. Either way, the place attracts a mixed bunch, who meet up, drink up, and inevitably move on.

Margarita Blue

C/Josep Anselm Clavé 6, 08002 (93 317 71 76). Metro Drassanes. **Open** 11am-2am Mon-Wed; 11am-3am Thur, Fri; 7pm-3am Sat; 7pm-2am Sun. **Credit** MC, V.
It must be the hot tunes that keep the punters coming back for more, because the quality of what you're being asked to believe is Mexican food seems to have been sacrificed in the name of expediency, and the so-called Margaritas (yes, they're blue) come from a Slush Puppie machine. Nonetheless, Margarita Blue remains a colourful and stylish bar-restaurant, which is always filled to capacity with a young (and especially foreign), party-going crowd.

Mesón del Café

C/Llibreteria 16, 08002 (93 315 07 54). Metro Jaume I.
Open 7am-9.30pm Mon-Sat. **No credit cards**.
This charming little (and we mean little) bar just off the
Plaça de Sant Jaume looks something like a miniature
Swiss chalet. Start your day at Mesón del Café with a
steaming cup of very good coffee accompanied by a
croissant, or toast and jam, and savour the moment at
one of its chunky wooden tables.

Nostromo

*C/Ripoll 16, 08002 (93 412 24 55). Metro Jaume I or
Urquinaona.* **Open** 2pm-2.30am Mon-Thur; 2pm-3am Fri;
8pm-3am Sat. **Credit** MC, V.
Named after the Conrad novel and run by a retired sailor,
this is a safe haven for landlubbers and mariners alike.
Chess sets are available, and shelves of mostly Spanish-
language books on the sea and exotic lands are
distributed about the bar. There's an excellent lunch
menu, and dinners are cooked to order (by advance
reservation only).

La Palma ★

*C/Palma de Sant Just 7, 08002 (93 315 06 56). Metro
Jaume I.* **Open** 8am-3.30pm, 7-10pm Mon-Thur; 8am-
3.30pm, 7-11pm Fri, Sat. **No credit cards**.

**Margarita
Blue** *(left)* has
a branch at
**El Taco de
Margarita**
Plaça Duc de
Mediniceli 1
(93 318
6321).

Café Zurich. See p55.

The assorted paintings lining the walls in this family-run bar are in fact originals by a group of artists – known as the Internos – who frequented the place in the 1950s. Don't expect to tap dance on the tables at La Palma – this is the kind of place that regulars come to for a quiet glass of wine, poured from one of the many barrels lining the walls, together with the easy-going familiarity that has served the establishment so well for nearly 70 years.

Pilé 43

C/Aglà 4, 08002 (93 317 39 02). Metro Liceu. **Open** 1.30-4.30pm, 7pm-2am Mon-Thur; 1.30-4.30pm, 7pm-3am Fri, Sat. **Credit** MC, V.

From the '70s vinyl chairs and smoked glass coffee tables to the lava lamps and the pendant light fittings, almost everything in this trendy Barcelona bar comes with a price tag attached. This is all well and good when there are plenty of people to give the place some atmosphere, but at quiet times, when custom is thin on the ground, there's no escaping the feeling that you're just drinking in a shop.

El Portalón

C/Banys Nous 20, 08002 (93 302 11 87). Metro Liceu.
Open 9am-midnight Mon-Sat. Closed Aug.
No credit cards.
While the rest of the Gothic quarter is busy modernising
and prettifying, this bodega remains untouched. As a
result, it has a faded, rundown feel as well as the still
discernible rustic charm of old. Created in the 1860s from
the stables of a medieval palace, it offers traditional tapas
and wine to its regulars, who sit chatting at wooden
booths under massive clusters of garlic.

Rabipelao

C/Mercè 26, 08002. Metro Drassanes. **Open** 8pm-2am
Mon-Thur, Sun; 8pm-3am Fri, Sat. **No credit cards**.
A tiny but friendly joint, with Andalucian tiling, and an
assortment of artistic junk hanging from the walls: a
bicycle wheel, the guts of a forgotten typewriter, rolls of
film, and dog-eared books. Intermittent projections slice
through the blood-red shadows deep at the back, while
smiling staff dole out cocktails and bocadillos to a mish-
mash of urban irregulars.

Schilling

C/Ferran 23, 08002 (93 317 67 87). Metro Liceu. **Open**
10am-1.30am Mon-Sat; noon-2.30am Sun. **Credit** V.
Spacious and utterly elegant – with a particularly large
gay clientele – this bar-café provides front-row seats for
watching the ebb and flow of humanity on the bustling
street outside. Schilling enjoyed a brief stint as 'the place
to be' when it opened a few years ago, but the beautiful
people have since grown restless and sashayed away.
Still, it is comfortable and popular, despite the famously
slow and surly service.

Shanghai

C/Aglà 9, 08002 (no phone). Metro Liceu. **Open** 7pm-3am
daily. **No credit cards**.
A saucy little mock-oriental drinking hole off
C/Escudellers that mixes down-at-heel glamour with
laid-back eccentricity. From the tasselled light fittings
to the shattered corner of the huge mirror, Shanghai is
scruffily beguiling, although the cocktails can take
forever to appear.

So_da

C/Avinyó 24, 08002 (93 412 27 76). Metro Liceu.
Open 9pm-2.30am Mon-Thur, Sun; 9pm-3am Fri, Sat.
No credit cards.
Once the high-fashion wares are safely locked up in the
great white wardrobes near the entrance, and the tubular
curtains of the changing room are twisted up out of the
way, a spruce clothes shop becomes a surprisingly scruffy
and comfortable bar, with a random selection of
seats, and decks on a trestle table in the corner: it can be
lively or laid-back, depending on the DJ.

Soniquete

*C/Milans 5, 08002 (639 382 354). Metro Drassanes or
Jaume I.* **Open** 9pm-3am Thur-Sun. **No credit cards**.
Pass through a doorway framed by a glass case packed
with plastic flowers and 'enter into a paradise of
flamenco', as they say. A candlelit bar with bits of kitsch
and strings of fairy lights plays host to homesick
Andalucians strumming their fingers raw on Thursday,
Friday and Saturday nights. If you're unlucky and no
one shows up to play or sing, it's still an atmospheric
place for a beer. If Soniquete catches on – the place
opened only in late 2001 – there are plans to open it
every night.

Travel Bar

*C/Boqueria 27, 08002 (93 342 52 52/
www.barcelonatravelbar.com). Metro Liceu.*
Open 9am-2am Mon-Thur, Sun; 9am-3am Fri, Sat.
No credit cards.

Wash down
the wonderful
ham with a
glass of wine
at one of the
little tables
crammed into
La Pineda
(C/Pi 16), a
charming old
grocery shop.

Pilé 43. *See p62.*

The ideal place for fun-seeking travellers to hook up to the internet (€1 for 15 minutes) or to hook up with friends. The helpful staff organise pub crawls, city tours (bicycle and walking) and weekend trips. The decor consists of slightly garish murals of planes swooping through the sky, or there are a few tables outside on a little square.

Venus Delicatessen

C/Avinyó 25, 08002 (93 301 15 85). Metro Liceu.
Open noon-midnight Mon-Sat. Closed 2wks Nov.
No credit cards.
This little café has a relaxed feel, with regularly changing displays of art on the walls, and plenty of newspapers and magazines. Light meals and salads are served from noon to midnight uninterrupted. Likewise, cool tunes play at all hours, attracting an international, young-spirited clientele.

La Vinateria del Call ★

C/Sant Domènec del Call 9, 08002 (93 302 60 92). Metro Jaume I or Liceu. **Open** 6pm-1am Mon-Sat.
Credit AmEx, DC, MC, V.
The narrow entrance to this deep llesqueria (*see p59* **Slices of Life**), furnished with dark wood and dusty bottles, has something of the Dickensian tavern about it, but once inside there's an eclectic music selection from sevillanas to rai, and lively multilingual staff. The wine list and range of hams and cheeses at La Vinateria del Call are outstanding; try the cecina de ciervo – wafer-thin slices of cured venison.

Xaloc

C/Palla 17, 08002 (93 301 19 90). Metro Liceu or Urquinaona. **Open** 9am-1am daily. **Credit** AmEx, DC, MC, V.
Huge glass windows display top-quality wines and foods; reproductions of Van Gogh and Klimt hang on the walls, and dozens of cured hams hang from the ceiling behind the chill cabinets. Not so long ago, the Zona Alta would have been the only location for this type of glossy café-delicatessen, but the times they are a-changin'.

Xocoa

C/Bot 4, 08002 (93 318 89 91). Metro Liceu. **Open** 10am-10pm Mon-Sat. **Credit** MC, V.
Sit at a low bar in retro, half egg-shaped chairs and watch the chefs prepare your crêpes. This spacious and modern café serves innovative meals and dessert samplers delivered in cutesy little glasses. The nearby branch on Petritxol, which serves more chocolate and less food, is more straightforward.

A branch of spacious, modern café **Xocoa** *(left)* can be found at C/Petritxol 11 (*93 301 1197*).

Raval

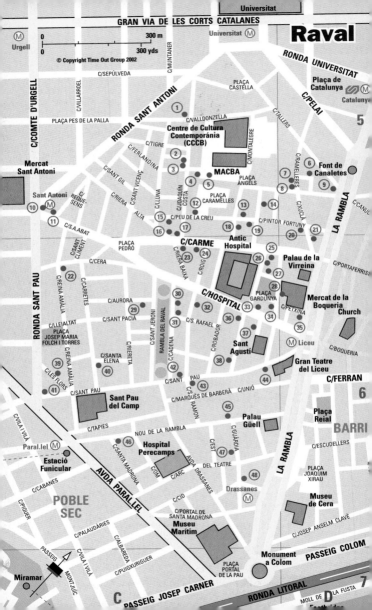

Ca l'Estevet. *See p70.*

Restaurants

Biblioteca

*C/Junta de Comerç 28, 08001 (93 412 6221). Metro
Liceu.* **Meals served** 1-4pm, 9pm-midnight Tue-Sat.
Average €€. **Credit** AmEx, DC, MC, V.

As its name suggests, this fresh, peaceful restaurant
houses a collection of gastronomic literature. Everything
from Elizabeth David to books on Zen cooking and pub
grub are presented for easy browsing in a decorative,
glass-doored bookcase. The menu isn't a bad read either,
and the unfussy dishes showcase the high-quality
ingredients: exquisite Galician oysters with Guinness,
golden pastry tartlets with Jabugo ham and prime beef
with Yorkshire pudding. There's also an unmissable
range of desserts and pastries. The fixed lunch menu is
dramatically cheaper (around €9) and offers more basic
fare such as pasta dishes and creative salads.

El Cafetí

C/Hospital 99 (end of passage), 08001 (93 329 24 19/
www.elcafeti.com). Metro Liceu. **Meals served** 1.30-
3.30pm, 9-11.30pm Tue-Sat; 1.30-3.30pm Sun. Closed 3wks
Aug. **Average** €€. **Credit** AmEx, DC, MC, V.
Tucked away in a Raval alley, this seductively cosy
restaurant evokes the sitting room of an elegant but
slightly batty old lady, and is said to be a favourite of
London mayor Ken Livingstone. Specialities include
paellas, mar i muntanya dishes, duck and venison. Menus
and staff are multilingual.

Ca l'Estevet

C/Valldonzella 46, 08001 (93 302 41 86). Metro
Universitat/ bus all routes to Plaça Universitat. **Meals**
served 1.30-4pm, 8.30-11pm Mon-Sat. Closed 2wks Aug.
Average €€. **Credit** AmEx, DC, MC, V.
In the '60s, Estevet was the place for writers, artists and
politicians – witness the signed photos and artistic
doodlings on the walls – and little has changed since. The
menu features the same filet de Café Paris served in a
buttery, herby sauce with wild mushrooms and succulent
cabrito (kid) that it always did. The food at times is
secondary to the atmosphere; starters can be spartan and
desserts tend towards the pre-packaged, but this is a
fabulously welcoming, relaxed place.

Hotel España. *See p77.*

Ca l'Isidre ★

C/Flors 12, 08001 (93 441 11 39/93 442 57 20). Metro Paral.lel. **Meals served** 1.30-4pm, 8.30-11.30pm Mon-Sat. Closed 2wks Aug. **Average** €€€€. **Credit** AmEx, DC, MC, V.

Isidre Gironés and his wife Montserrat have taken their modest idea of a family-run restaurant to vertiginous heights, offering one of Spain's most consistent top-flight gourmet menus, and counting royalty among their clientele. The secret of their success has been to draw the maximum potential out of high-quality market-bought ingredients, which are served in disarmingly straightforward dishes. Catalan, Spanish and European classics, featuring shellfish, magnificent local lamb, or fine foie gras, throw out an ongoing challenge to the diner: have you ever tasted anything better? The kitchen handles seafood masterfully, whether it's Atlantic angulas (eels) or a tuna fillet, and knowledgeable wine recommendations enhance the dining experience. Only Ca l'Isidre's closing course breaks the tendency towards understatement, with daughter and master pastry cook Núria (soon to be director as her parents hint at retirement) elaborating some of the most deliciously creative desserts imaginable. The chocolate mousse is an awesome achievement.

Can Lluis *p72* has a branch at **Els Ocellets**, Ronda Sant Pau 55, Barri Gòtic (93 441 1046).

Can Lluís

C/Cera 49, 08001 (93 441 11 87). Metro Sa€nt Antoni or Paral.lel. **Meals served** 1.30-4pm, 8.30-11.30pm Mon-Sat. Closed 4wks Aug, Sept. **Average** €€.
Credit AmEx, DC, MC, V.

This restaurant has the same menu as its sister, Els Ocellets (just a minute's walk away on the other side of the Ronda), and is equally popular, but has bags more atmosphere. Try the spicy romesco salad made with ground nuts, peppers, tomatoes and anchovies or the hearty estofat (stew). Bookings are only taken for groups, so get there early to avoid having to wait.

La Casa de la Rioja ★

C/Peu de la Creu 8-10, 08001 (93 443 33 63). Metro Catalunya. **Meals served** 1-4pm, 8.30-11pm Mon-Sat. **Average** €. **Credit** MC, V.

This cultural centre for La Rioja incorporates a restaurant showcasing the cuisine of the region. A flash-looking place, it looks incongruous in this slightly shabby part of town, but provides some of the best value food in Barcelona. There are great salads on offer (try crab and salmon), cazuelitos (little terracotta dishes of stews) and other hearty fare, all eclipsed by the ambrosial desserts, which include own-made chocolate and pistachio ice-cream and an inspired roquefort cheesecake. The lunchtime set menu is a real bargain – for the price of a bottle of wine, you get three courses of such delights *and* a bottle of wine.

Casa Leopoldo

C/Sant Rafael 24, 08001 (93 441 69 42). Metro Liceu. **Meals served** 1.30-4pm, 9-11pm Tue-Sat; 1.30-4pm Sun. Closed Aug. **Average** €€€. **Credit** AmEx, DC, MC, V.

This friendly family restaurant opened in the 1930s, and time seems to have stood still ever since. Bullfighting paraphernalia, wooden fittings and azulejos (tiles) give plenty of old-style charm, and traditional food is still the order of the day with generous and excellent seafood, steaks and homey stews. It seems the only thing to have moved with the times is the bill, which can become almost futuristic if you order the fish of the day.

El Convent

C/Jerusalem 3, 08001 (93 317 10 52). Metro Liceu. **Meals served** 1-4pm, 8pm-midnight Mon-Sat. **Average** €€. **Credit** AmEx, DC, MC, V.

A convivial restaurant, with handsome antique fittings and enjoyable food. The menu is traditional Catalan – highlights include interesting game dishes such as estofado de jabalí (wild boar stew) and solomillo de ciervo (venison steak). Be prepared to take a seat and wait, particularly at lunchtime.

A new and stylish shop selling delicious cakes, quiches and empanadas is **Agualaboca** (C/Pintor Fortuny, 34). It also has more hearty fare to take away.

La Boqueria

Part market, part theatre, La Boqueria (also known as the Mercat de Sant Josep) has some of the most frequently photographed vegetables in Europe, the most persistently fugitive crayfish and the most vigilant stall-holders. Recently refurbished to make it more accessible and airy, this is the biggest and best of Spanish markets. Established on La Rambla in 1836, it's open from Monday to Saturday from 6am to 9pm (though if you're trying to buy things at lunchtime, you might have to nudge a stall-holder from her siesta).

The most extravagant displays are by the entrance, acting as a honey trap for passing visitors, with exotic fruit and vegetables, and rainbows of candied fruit. Prices here are higher than inside – partly because much of the fruit is imported, and available regardless of the season. Further in, you get what you pay for, with price and quality varying from stall to stall. There are fruit and vegetable stalls, meat, bread and egg stalls, a wine shop and even a pharmacy (should you overdo it in the wine shop). At the centre, the circle of fish stalls is an amphitheatre of ice and excitement as the unflagging crustaceans try to escape. Around these is a handful of stalls selling cured fish, especially salt cod. You can buy it stiff and salted to pack in your suitcase, or pre-bathed in marble basins to remove the salt.

A couple of stalls sell the bits of meat others throw away: livers, entrails and sheep heads, with eyes that watch you as you make your purchase. For the gourmet, there is game (on the left, as you enter) fresh in season and frozen all year round, including hare, boar and that well-known Catalan indigent, ostrich. You might want to cook it with wild mushrooms – Llorenç Petràs, at the far end, often has over two dozen varieties of fresh and dried funghi, as well as bunches of fresh herbs, wild strawberries and other treasures of the forest.

And finally, you can survey your purchases over market-fresh tapas at one of the bars inside; Kiosko Pinotxo, by the entrance, also serves sturdy Catalan stews as well as a variety of toasted sandwiches. On Fridays and Saturdays, you can finish shopping in style with cava and oysters.

Déu n'hi do

C/Nou de la Rambla 95, 08001 (93 441 98 28). Metro Paral.lel. **Meals served** 1-4.30pm Mon-Sat. Closed 2wks Aug. **Average** €. **No credit cards**.

The Catalan name (an expression of surprise) is misleading; this is an Argentine restaurant, with a fixed-price lunch menu. Jovial curly-haired owner Chus offers a fine churrasco (barbecued steak) with chimichurri (garlic sauce). Chus loves to explain how the quiche-like corn pie was his mother's recipe, or how the tender octopus in the pulpo gallego was caught locally by a neighbour. Service is sometimes slow, and you may have to provide a gentle reminder to bring on the next course. There are interesting desserts and good coffee.

Elisabets

C/Elisabets 2-4, 08001 (93 317 58 26). Metro Catalunya. **Meals served** 7.30am-10pm Mon-Thur, Sat; 7.30am-2am Fri. Closed 3wks Aug. **Average** €. **No credit cards**.

An unpretentious, friendly place to have lunch among the denizens of the Raval and those on their way back from the MACBA. Traditional Catalan dishes are decent value, and a jumble of old radios and other eccentric touches make this preferable to most of the cheapies hereabouts.

La Fragua

Rambla del Raval 15, 08001 (93 442 80 97). Metro Liceu or Sant Antoni. **Meals served** 1-4pm, 8pm-1am Tue-Sun. **Average** €. **Credit** AmEx, DC, MC, V.

In a city obsessed with style and design, La Fragua is an oddity, a spit and sawdust village restaurant complete with nicotine walls, stone floor and the forge that gives it its name. This is rural simplicity incarnate, serving food to match. On offer are salads, stews, steaks and sausages, with a brief vegetarian section consisting of omelettes and delicious spinach rolls with pinenuts and raisins. It's a good budget option, especially in summer, when there are tables out on the lively Rambla del Raval. The nighttime menu is good value at €8.5 (without wine).

Lupino. *See p77.*

If you want to deeply know Barcelona begin with
Margarita Blue & Rita Blue
Let yourself be abducted by this city

La Gardunya

C/Jerusalem 18, 08001 (93 302 43 23). Metro Liceu.
Meals served 1-4pm, 8pm-1am Mon-Sat. **Average** €.
Credit AmEx, DC, MC, V.

A tall, thin, glass and steel building, funkily decorated,
with a mosaic of stone and sand set into the floor and a
colourful spiral staircase leading up to a mezzanine.
Grab a table up there to get a view into bustling La
Boqueria market (*see p73* **La Boqueria**, and watch
your sardinas or manitas de cabrito (kid's trotters) being
haggled over. La Gardunya is a much livelier spot at
lunchtime (with both market workers and customers)
than at night.

Hotel España

C/Sant Pau 9, 08001 (93 318 17 58). Metro Liceu. **Meals
served** 1-4pm, 8.30pm-midnight daily. **Average** €€.
Credit AmEx, DC, MC, V.

The standard of cooking in the restaurant of the Hotel
España unfortunately falls short of its Modernista interior,
which has floral tiled mosaics and an impressive ceiling
conceived by architect Domènech i Montaner in 1902.
Seafood is the speciality, in tune with the Ramon Casas
underwater murals in the back dining room, although even
the chef's recommendations can disappoint. Filo pastry
stuffed with cod mousse and shrimp wasn't exactly cold, it
just tasted as if it hadn't been fully defrosted. The monkfish
ragoût came inexplicably pan-fried. The €8 menu is
perhaps a lower-risk way to bask in the splendid decor.

Lupino

C/Carme 33, 08001 (93 442 80 97). Metro Liceu. **Meals
served** 1-4pm, 9pm-midnight Mon-Wed; 1-4pm, 9pm-2am
Thur-Sat; 1-4pm, 9pm-midnight Sun. **Average** €€.
Credit AmEx, MC, V.

Sky-high production values and a slick public relations job
mean that this restaurant-cocktail bar has been packed
since it opened in early 2002. All your fusion favourites –
such as lamb with couscous or chicken with ginger and
sesame, with the odd nod to traditional Spanish cooking
(stir-fried vegetables with strips of membrillo) – are here.
They're also surprisingly cheap and tasty. Lupino
embodies so much of what makes Barcelona Barcelona
that it is sure to spawn a thousand imitations. When a rash
of retro-futuristic airport lounges with yellow leatherette
banquettes, ambient soundtracks and waiters dressed like
mortuary attendants hits the city, don't forget that you
heard it here first.

Mama Café

*C/Doctor Dou 10, 08001 (93 301 29 40). Metro
Catalunya or Liceu.* **Meals served** 1-5pm Mon;
1pm-1am Tue-Sat. **Average** €. **Credit** DC, MC, V.

For
spectacular
sandwiches
and an
aromatic
cornucopia
of breads,
including
soya, nine-
grain, olive
and Finnish,
head for
Forn Boix
(C/Xuclà 23).

Pla dels Àngels

Very much of its barri, with Rajasthani wall hangings and slide projections, the Mama Café offers Mediterranean dishes, such as salmon in rosemary oil, or warm goat's cheese salad with pear vinaigrette. Staff are charming.

Mesón David
C/Carretas 63, 08001 (93 441 59 34). Metro Paral.lel.
Meals served 1-4pm, 8pm-midnight Mon, Tue, Thur-Sun. Closed Aug. **Average** €. **Credit** AmEx, MC, V.
Ordering can be a lottery, but pulpo gallego (octopus Galician-style), trucha navarra (whole trout stuffed with serrano ham and cheese) or lechazo (tender-roasted pork knuckle) are safe bets. Prices are absurdly low.

Pla dels Àngels ★
C/Ferlandina 23, 08001 (93 329 40 47). Metro Universitat. **Meals served** 1.30-4pm Mon; 1.30-4pm, 9-11pm Tue-Thur; 1.30-4pm, 9pm-midnight Fri, Sat. **Average** €. **Credit** DC, MC, V.
Pla dels Àngels is artistically decorated, and buzzes with conversation. A short menu comprises imaginative salads, great spaghetti and gnocchi, carpaccios of duck, salmon or octopus and a few meat dishes (try chicken with tiger

Buenas Migas
p52 offers wonderful focaccia, cakes and crumbles, as does its similar sister café on Plaça Bonsuccès 6, Raval (93 319 1380).

nut sauce). Prices are reasonable for what is often excellent cooking. Restaurants from the same stable include **Coses de Menjar** *(see p101)* and **Semproniana** *(see p136)*.

Sagarra

C/Xuclà 9, 08001 (93 301 06 04). Metro Liceu. **Open** 1-11pm Tue-Sun. **Average** €. **Credit** AmEx, DC, MC, V.
Sagarra opened in the spring, with a top value lunchtime menu. Less than €8 gets you asparagus with romesco sauce, followed by pork with sobrassada (spicy Mallorcan sausage) and a pudding. A la carte options include a la brasa dishes among them rabbit, quail and kid, or duck served with bittersweet tomato confit.

Silenus

C/Àngels 8, 08001 (93 302 26 80). Metro Liceu. **Meals served** 1.30-4pm, 8.30-11.45pm Mon-Sat. **Average** €€.
Credit DC, MC, V.
Silenus offers a stunning selection of dishes, mainly modern Catalan but drawing on the vogue for all things Japanese. Simple classics are given a twist; crema verde de guisantes (pea soup), for example, is served with lime ice-cream and pancetta. Service can be infuriatingly relaxed.

International

Fil Manila

*C/Ramelle~res 3, 08001 (93 318 64 87). Metro
Catalunya.* **Meals served** 11.30am-4.30pm, 8-11.30pm
Mon, Wed-Sun. **Average** €. **No credit cards**.
A staggering menu (over 100 dishes) is divided into
grilled, barbecue, sizzling, rice and noodle dishes. Fil
Manila was until recently the city's only Filipino
restaurant, and is still the best, with a great selection of
dishes, such as sautéed jackfruit with shrimp and coconut
milk, and meat and fish cooked on sizzling stone platters.
At teatime (4-8pm), there are lighter merienda dishes.

Snack attack

Spanish Tapas

The Spanish tapa (meaning
'lid') was originally a saucer
that innkeepers garnished with
tit-bits from the kitchen, and
placed on top of the drink
offered to coachmen when they
stopped at inns. The tradition
took hold and tapas are now
prepared in a thousand
combinations, including whole
mushrooms fried in white wine
and garlic (champiñones al
ajillo), prawns and garlic
(gambas al ajillo), battered
squid rings (chocos), steamed

clams with garlic and
parsley (almejas al
vapor), octopus
(pulpo) and little
green peppers
(pimientos del
padrón) that are a
kind of culinary
Russian roulette –
not all are hot, but
one or two have a
vicious bite. Look out
for bombas; huge
potato and meat
croquettes served
with a fiery sauce.
    Barcelona also has
hundreds of tiny,
brightly lit snack and
sandwich bars that
serve food in smaller
portions (raciones),

Punjab Restaurante

C/Joaquín Costa 1B (93 443 38 99). Metro Liceu.
Meals served 11am-midnight daily. **Average** €.
No credit cards.

Absurdly cheap and gloriously, unintentionally kitsch (those absurd-looking tablecloths are the real thing), Punjab Restaurante offers a salad, curry with rice and naan and a pudding for an unbeatably good value €3.60. Anyone who is prepared to go the extra euro is rewarded with a wider and more tempting choice of dishes involving tandooris, birianis and couscous dishes. A recent Latin liaison in the kitchen has brought about an incongruous list of South American dishes, in addition to the standard menu.

but which don't qualify as tapas bars. They offer some of the typical, less elaborate and cheaper Spanish dishes, such as tortilla (omelette), patatas bravas (fried potatoes in a spicy red sauce and/or garlic mayonnaise), snails (caracoles) or pork skewers (pinchos morunos).

Catalan Llesques

Catalonia has its own style of snack food equivalent to tapas, called llesques. Cold meats, pâtés and cheeses are usually accompanied by pa amb tomàquet (bread with tomato), a tradition hailing from leaner years when stale bread was made softer by smearing tomato on to it. See *p57*, **Slices of life**.

Basque Pintxos

Basque bars are usually quite open, rustic, wood and stone affairs with stools and standing space around the bar. They are known for their pintxos, small pieces of bread topped with some ingenious culinary combination. These include anchovies, pâté de Roquefort, cured ham, black pudding (morcilla), croquettes of chicken or ham, dates wrapped in bacon, small roast red peppers filled with tuna, quails' eggs, spicy peppers and, naturally, tortilla.

Each pintxo is impaled by a toothpick, which you should keep on your plate, so that the barman knows how many you have had. Trays of pintxos are generally brought out at certain hours, often midday and 7pm.

Shalimar

C/Carme 71, 08001 (93 329 34 96). Metro Liceu.
Meals served 1-4pm, 8-11.30pm Mon; 8-11.30pm Tue;
1-4pm, 8-11.30pm Wed-Sun. **Average** €. **Credit** MC, V.
Homesick Brits (and, indeed, Pakistanis) will feel right at
home at Shalimar, with its short but adequate selection of
Madras and tandoori dishes, birianis and a tame vindaloo.
The restaurant's nothing fancy in terms of decor and
atmosphere – don't go expecting plate-warmers with tea
lights or bottles of Kingfisher, and there's a TV competing
with the stereo in the corner – but it does the job well
enough considering the fairly limited resources that
Barcelona offers for this kind of oriental food. Even the
wallpaper makes a plucky attempt at red flock.

Vegetarian

Biocenter

C/Pintor Fortuny 25, 08001 (93 301 45 83). Metro Liceu.
Meals served 1-5pm Mon-Sat. **Average** €. **No credit
cards.**
Biocenter has expanded from the back room of a health-
food shop to a restaurant in its own right situated directly
across the road. It's one of the few vegan-friendly
restaurants in town and serves an impressive range of
imaginative salads along with dishes such as mushroom
tart or spinach parcels, which come with a heap of brown
rice and sauces, and delicious organic beers.

Silenus. *See p79.*

L'Hortet

C/Pintor Fortuny 32, 08001 (93 317 61 89). Metro Liceu. **Meals served** 1.15-4pm, 8.30-11pm Mon-Wed; 8.30-11pm Thur-Sun. **Average** €. **Credit** MC, V.

The chatty waitresses and homey decor make l'Hortet one of the most welcoming vegetarian restaurants in Barcelona, and the big stacks of papers and health magazines positively encourage you to linger once your meal is finished. For starters you can generally choose from a soup or heavier dishes such as couscous with ratatouille, but if appetite's a problem there's always the small but well-dressed salad buffet. The hefty main courses are guaranteed to put you into a carbohydrate coma before long – take your pick from spinach cannelloni with vegetable croquettes, or giant, tomatoey enchiladas under a mattress of melted cheese. Thankfully, desserts are light and fruity. The gist of the rather long-winded, inspirational message posted on the restaurant's windows is that no smoking is allowed.

Sésamo

C/Sant Antoni Abat 52, 08001 (93 441 6411). Metro Sant Antoni. **Meals served** 1.30-4pm Mon; 1.30-4pm, 9-11.30pm Wed-Sun. Closed Aug. **Average** €. **Credit** MC, V.

Within a tomato's toss of the Sant Antoni market is this new, fresh and friendly vegetarian restaurant. The two-course lunch menu consists of excellent soups, salads,

La Confitería. *See p88.*

lasagnes, quiches and rice dishes. At night a healthy range of à la carte dishes might include crêpes stuffed with sautéd vegetables or gnocchetti with tomato, onion and ricotta. The wine list at Sésamo is not extensive but decent. Mornings, there's muesli, fresh juices and own-made cakes on offer. Music tends toward trendy, mellow electronica, and the decor is marked by an orderly grove of tall, bamboo-like lamps that lean over diners in the main room.

Cafés & Bars

Aurora

C/Aurora 7, 08001 (93 442 30 44). Metro Paral.lel.
Open 8pm-3am Mon-Fri; 6am-noon, 8pm-3am Fri, Sat.
Admission €3 6am-noon Fri, Sat. **No credit cards.**

Since the Rambla del Raval opened up, it's been easier to find this idiosyncratic little bar, but style-wise it's still off the beaten track, with murals and fittings that have been following their own weird evolution for years. The many arty/creative/unkempt regulars can appear cliquey, but it's basically friendly, with seats in the cosy loft space upstairs.

Bar Bodega Fortuny

C/Pintor Fortuny 31, 08001 (93 317 98 92). Metro Catalunya. **Open** 10am-12.30am Tue-Sun. Closed 1wk Aug. **No credit cards.**

The design elements here include white walls with colourfully painted pop-art circles, a playful mural of Bacchus-inspired dancing bottles, and some retro lamps. The end result is a bar that is as laid-back as its faithful regulars, who might spend hours here playing chess or chatting over a healthy meal. Popular with gay women.

Raval

Bar Kasparo ★

Plaça Vicenç Martorell 4, 08001 (93 302 20 72/
www.kasparo.com). Metro Catalunya. **Open** *Summer*
9am-midnight daily. *Winter* 9am-10pm daily. Closed Jan.
No credit cards.
Located under the high arcade of this sunny, traffic-free
plaça, there are few places this peaceful in the heart of
Barcelona's Old City. The bar is friendly, Australian-
run and serves a mean chicken salad. Almost all the
seating is outside, so it's an ideal spot for soaking up
the sun throughout the spring and summer.

Bar Mendizábal ★

C/Junta de Comerç 2 (no phone). Metro Liceu. **Open**
8am-midnight daily. **No credit cards.**
This is a tiny place with no more than a colourful little
bar and awning. You can stand on the pavement or sit in
the scenic square just across the street to be served. For
most of the last century, Bar Mendizábal was a popular
workers' hangout. Recently reopened, it draws a mix of
local workers and culturally savvy patrons, who come to
enjoy the fresh juices, milkshakes, inventive sandwiches
and what are probably the best tortillas in town, made
by the owner's grandmother.

Bar Muy Buenas

C/Carme 63, 08001 (93 442 50 53). **Open** 4pm-2.30am
Mon-Thur; 4pm-3am Fri, Sat; 5.30pm-2.30am Sun. **Credit**
MC, V.
Swooping Modernista woodwork, a marble bar
(originally a trough for salting cod) and the original beer
taps – one side for the barman to pull pints, the other
for customers to help themselves to water – have
remained in this welcoming little split-level bar.
Friendly staff serve falafel, houmous, lentil soup and
own-made cakes in the evenings, and there are poetry
readings on Wednesdays.

Bar Pastís

C/Santa Mònica 4, 08001 (93 318 79 80). Metro
Drassanes. **Open** 7.30pm-2.30am Mon-Thur; 7.30pm-
3.30am Fri, Sat; 7.30pm-2.30am Sun. **Credit** AmEx, MC, V.
A larger-than-life papier-mâché woman, grinning
drunkenly and clutching a drink in one hand and a
cigarette in the other, is suspended from the ceiling of
this attractive and very quirky little bar. It was opened
in the 1940s by Quimet and Carme, a Catalan couple
who'd lived in Marseilles, and the pictures on the walls
were painted by Quimet himself, apparently always
when drunk. The current management at Bar Pastís is
upholding the traditions established by this bohemian
pair by continuing to play exclusively French music and
serving pastis and absinthe.

Bar Ra

*Plaça de la Gardunya 3, 08001 (93 423 18 78). Metro
Liceu.* **Open** 1.30-4pm, 9pm-midnight Mon-Sat. **Credit**
AmEx, DC, MC, V.

A better name couldn't have been chosen for this
happening bar in the square behind the Boqueria market.
Ra was the sun god, and sun is what this large terrace
receives year-round (large, colourful umbrellas provide
shade in summer). Foreigners craving something more
than the standard croissant for breakfast will be
delighted by the bacon, eggs, toast, juice, muesli, yoghurt
and oatmeal on offer. Lunch and dinner ranges from
Mexican to Thai to West Indian fare, served to the beat
of drum 'n' bass, ambient, jazz or whatever suits the
prevailing mood.

Bar 68/The Kitchen BCN

C/Sant Pau 68, 08001 (93 441 31 15). Metro Paral.lel.
Open *Bar* 8pm-2am Tue-Thur; 8pm-3am Fri, Sat.
Restaurant 9pm-midnight Tue-Sat. **No credit cards**.
The charm of this candlelit place comes from its stripped-
down style, and its emulation of a clandestine after-hours
bar. A row of glowing orange lamps made from recycled
water bottles hangs over the bar, there are slide
projections on the wall and a DJ plays mellow modern
music. Dinner is also served (perhaps the reason the bar
has two names).

Benidorm

*C/Joaquín Costa 39, 08001 (93 317 80 52). Metro
Universitat/bus all routes to Plaça Universitat.* **Open**
7pm-2am Mon-Thur; 7pm-2.30am Fri, Sat; 7pm-2am Sun.
No credit cards.
A sunken sitting room behind a glass front, flock
wallpaper, charity-shop souvenirs and granny-chic: this
could be a 22nd-century antiquarian's confused
reconstruction of the way we used to live. With pop/
electronic DJs and an intriguing mix of foreigners and
home-turf dudes, the smoky atmosphere is usually
buzzing; if you're lucky you may even find a seat in the
small back lounge.

Boadas

C/Tallers 1, 08001 (93 318 95 92). Metro Catalunya.
Open noon-2am Mon-Thur; noon-3am Fri, Sat.
No credit cards.
This tiny cocktail bar is difficult to spot, but it doesn't
need a neon sign as locals know where it is. In the height
of summer, when crowds converge on La Rambla, this
1930s institution, with its slick, black-jacketed barmen,
is a cool, civilised oasis. The daytime clientele are usually
well dressed and elderly, while the night-time patrons are
a livelier, more varied bunch.

For late-night
beer runs,
there's
nowhere
better than
Champion (La
Rambla 113),
a huge and
well-stocked
supermarket
open until
10pm
every night.

Casa Almirall

C/Joaquín Costa 33, 08001 (no phone). Metro Universitat.
Open 7pm-2.30am Mon-Thur; 7pm-3am Fri, Sat.
No credit cards.
Opened in 1860, the Almirall is the oldest continuously
functioning bar in the city. It still has its elegant early
(and charmingly unkempt) Modernista woodwork. Iron
beams supporting the original wooden crossbeams are
the result of city-enforced renovations. The big soft sofas
have been allowed to stay.

La Concha

C/Guàrdia 14, 08001 (93 302 41 18). Metro Drassanes.
Open 4pm-3am daily. **No credit cards.**
The sequins, slingbacks, pathos and paunches of the
Raval's surviving drag cabaret scene live on down the
street in transvestite bar El Cangrejo, but occasionally
make an appearance here at La Concha, amid the myriad
faces – from '60s sex kitten to kohl-eyed diva – of Spanish
screen and drag icon Sara Montiel. The cobwebs have
been dusted off and the wilted flowers replaced to attract
a gay-friendly but very mixed new crowd. The bar is at
its liveliest at weekends when there's energetic dancing
on the chequered tiles to a mix of rai, flamenco and live
bands. There are also gigs from midnight to 2am on
Fridays and Sundays.

La Confitería

C/Sant Pau 128, 08001 (93 443 04 58). Metro Paral.lel.
Open 6pm-3am Mon-Sat; 6pm-2am Sun. **No credit cards.**
A friendly hangout, charmingly done up with old
chandeliers, Modernista wood panelling and murals of
rural scenes dating from the 1920s. It's a popular bar
attracting a wide cross-section of people.

Escribà

La Rambla 83, 08002 (93 301 60 27). Metro Liceu.
Open 8.30am-9pm daily. **Credit** (over €9) MC, V.
If you think this lovely Modernista façade with its
colourful mosaic tiles is a treat in itself, just wait until
you sample some of the own-made chocolates and
pastries inside. They also sell local moscatell wine in cute,
decorative bottles and have a handful of tables outside in
the shade of a narrow street.

Granja M Viader

*C/Xuclà 4-6, 08001 (93 318 34 86). Metro Liceu or
Catalunya.* **Open** 5-8.45pm Mon; 9am-1.45pm, 5-8.45pm
Tue-Sat. Closed 1wk Aug. **Credit** MC, V.
A pavement plaque commemorates this cafe's 130-plus
years of service as a granja (literally, farm), specialising in
dairy products and suizos (thick hot chocolate topped with
whipped cream). You can sample mel i mató (curd cheese

Granja M Viader

with honey) at one of the marble-topped tables, while
sitting with the mainly elderly locals. Local honey, cheese,
meat or chocolate are also available to take away.

Horiginal

*C/Ferlandina 29, 08001 (93 443 39 98). Metro Sant
Antoni.* **Open** 8.30pm-2.30am Mon-Thur; 8.30pm-3am Fri,
Sat. **Credit** MC, V.
A colourful new café by the MACBA, Horiginal is warm
and relaxed, with shelves of poetry, art exhibitions,
excellent music (jazz, flamenco) and a mix of clients laid-

back locals and book-reading travellers. The tables outside offer a view of the museum and square, and there's a good Mediterranean menu at lunch. On Thursday and Fridays at 10pm, poetry readings and small concerts are held.

Iposa Bar

C/Floristes de la Rambla 14, 08001 (93 318 60 86/www.bariposa.com). Metro Liceu. **Open** 1pm-3am Mon-Sat. **Credit** MC, V.

Iposa is fresh, cool and colourful. Art photos are projected on to a huge burlap screen on a back wall, and the house DJ might play anything from Cuban rhythms to ambient

Marsella. *See p92.*

and house. Excellent meals are served at both lunch and dinner, along with yummy own-made tapas. There are also tables outside on a pleasant, leafy square.

London Bar

C/Nou de la Rambla 34, 08001 (93 318 52 61). Metro Liceu. **Open** 7.30pm-4.30am Tue-Thur; 7pm-5am Fri, Sat; 7.30pm-4.30am Sun. Closed 2wks Aug. **Credit** MC, V.
The London Bar hasn't changed its extravagant look since it opened in 1910. It's popular among young expats and party-going Barcelonins. There are regular gigs (no entrance fee), but note that drink prices go up accordingly.

Marsella

C/Sant Pau 65, 08001 (93 442 72 63). Metro Liceu. **Open** 10pm-2am Mon-Thur; 10pm-3am Fri, Sat. **No credit cards**.
A well-loved bar that's been in the same family for five generations. It's said that Jean Genet used to come here, attracted, no doubt, by the locally made absinthe, which is still stocked. Dusty, untapped 100-year-old bottles sit in tall glass cabinets, old mirrors line the walls, and assorted chandeliers loom over the cheerful, largely foreign crowd.

Merry Ant ★

C/Peu de la Creu 23, 08001 (no phone). Metro Sant Antoni. **Open** 8pm-2am Tue-Sun. **No credit cards**.
The bizarre and slightly unhinged work of a rebellious carpenter, the Merry Ant is both a bar and a 'cultural association'. Local artist Toto has sawed, hammered and glued a collection of found objects into a remarkable, Frankenstein-like vision of interior design. Soft red lighting helps the bar's easy-going arty crowd to unwind.

Muebles Navarro

C/Riera Alta 4-6, 08001 (no phone). Metro Sant Antoni. **Open** 6pm-midnight Tue-Thur; 6pm-3am Fri, Sat; 6pm-midnight Sun. **No credit cards**.
There's more room in this café (a former furniture shop) than its owners know what to do with, so they've stuffed it with mismatched old chairs, sofas and lamps. The result is a funky, original space, with plenty of comfortable places to relax and enjoy the excellent New York cheesecake.

Rita Blue

Plaça Sant Agustí 3, 08001 (93 412 34 38). Metro Liceu. **Open** noon-2am Mon-Wed, Sun; noon-3am Thur-Sat. **Credit** AmEx, DC, MC, V.
The food is affordable Mexican, although you may find yourself whacking on more chilli, but the place to cradle a blue Margarita is downstairs in El Sotano, where there are chairs to slump in and room to dance to full-belly-friendly deep house grooves. Occasionally, there are Latin bands.

La Italiana (C/Bon Succès 12) holds all the ingredients you need to enjoy la dolce vita: grappas, Italian wines, cheeses and wonderful fresh pasta.

Merry Ant

Raval

La Ruta de los Elefantes

C/Hospital 48, 08001 (93 301 16 81). Metro Liceu.
Open 8.30pm-2.30am Mon-Thur; 8.30pm-3am Fri, Sat.
No credit cards.

Behind the wrought-ironwork of the arabesque double doors, La Ruta is a self-regulating enclave for a raggle-taggle mix of travellers, students and street characters, plus the odd off-duty living statue in silver paint. Indeterminately ethnic and definitely alternative, djembes and didgeridoos with an earthy Latin flavour get the dreadlocks swinging at the back on live music nights. You can cool off with own-made ice-cream on the way out.

Els Tres Tombs

Ronda Sant Antoni 2, 08001 (93 443 41 11). Metro Sant Antoni. **Open** 6am-2am daily. **No credit cards.**

Not a graveyard in sight; the bar's morbid-sounding name, Els Tres Tombs, refers, in fact, to 'the three circuits' of the area performed by a procession of men on horseback during the Catalan Festa dels Tres Tombs in January. This lively bar and restaurant has a great selection of tapas. Its sunny outside terrace is always busy, but especially during the Sunday book market at the nearby Mercat Sant Antoni.

Stylish Mexican restaurant/bar **Margarita Blue** *p60* has a branch at **Rita Blue** Plaça Sant Agustí 3 (93 412 3438).

The best breakfasts

The Bagel Shop
(see p47).

Bar Kasparo
(see p86).

Bar Ra
(see p87).

Café del Born
(see p117).

Laie Libreria Café
(see p152).

La Palma
(see p61).

Els Tres Tombs
(see above).

La Ribera

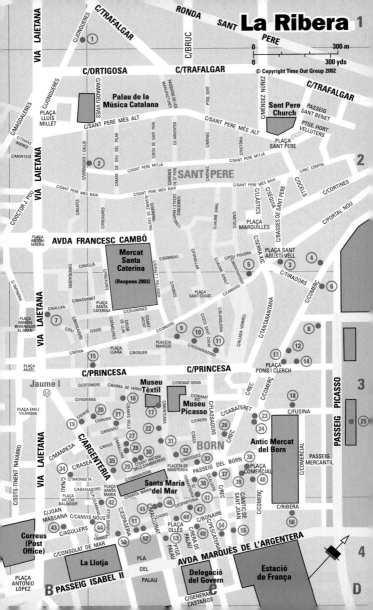

Restaurants

Abac ★

C/Rec 79-89, 08003 (93 319 66 00). Metro Barceloneta.
Meals served 8.30-10.30pm Mon; 1.30-3.30pm, 8.30-
10.30pm Tue-Sat. Closed 2wks Aug. **Average** €€€€.
Credit AmEx, DC, MC, V.

Stepping into Abac is like stepping into an IKEA photo
shoot through which immaculate waiters clad in dark-
grey Nehru jackets pace endlessly. The blond wood, bare
walls and unfussy furniture provide the perfect
unobtrusive backdrop to some elaborate dishes and
impeccable service. Almost everyone orders the menú
degustación: an absurdly indulgent series of dishes
normally involving several types of fish, a meat dish, a
cheese course and two puddings. On our visit tuna with
broccoli cream and caviar wrestled for supremacy with
langoustine on a bed of couscous served with artichoke
crisps. Scallops with braised endive and wild mushroom
sauce came close. The only disappointment (and
standards by this point are sky-high) are the puddings:
a bland selection of milk-based desserts not greatly suited
to rounding off a heavy meal. Better to taste some of the
superb cheeses and hold out for the petits fours.

Arrel

C/Fusina 5, 08003 (93 319 92 99). Metro Arc de Triomf.
Open 1-4pm, 8pm-midnight Tue-Sat; 1-4pm Sun.
Average €€. **Credit** AmEx, DC, MC, V.

A new venture, in the platito/designer tapas mould, Arrel
has a list of dishes 'para picar' (to nibble at), and then a
few more fortifying fish dishes. The fish is generally
good, but there's more fun to be had in sharing a selection
of little treats, which might include foie with caramelised
pineapple and watercress; lamb cutlets with romesco
sauce and all i oli sweetened with membrillo; or tuna
tataki with sesame and citrus dressing. Maybe because
the place is finding its feet, the staff are very keen to
please, and the chef genuinely interested in what you
think. This, combined with the smart but trendy design
and funky world electronica played low, make Arrel a
very welcome addition to the Born's restaurant scene.

Bar Salvador

*C/Canvis Nous 8, 08003 (93 310 10 41). Metro
Barceloneta or Jaume I.* **Meals served** 9am-5pm Mon-
Fri. **Average** €. **Credit** MC, V.

This bustling family-run restaurant is ruled by Pepita,
who supplies the hectic dining room from an impossibly
small kitchen. She dishes up excellent Catalan food for
local workers while keeping an eagle eye on the bar's

La Ribera

Cal Pep

good-natured waiters and treating them to occasional rebukes of the kind only family members could tolerate. The food is always affordable and good – favourites include pollastre amb crema d'ametlles (chicken with almonds) and jarret de vedella rostit (knuckle of veal). The fish specials are also superb. This is a no-frills place that is sunny, relaxed and unfailingly friendly.

Brasserie Flo

C/Jonqueres 10, 08003 (93 319 31 02). Metro Urquinaona. **Meals served** 1.30-4pm, 8pm-12.30am Mon-Thur; 1.30-4pm, 8pm-1am Fri, Sat; 1.30-4pm, 8pm-12.30am Sun. **Average** €. **Credit** AmEx, DC, MC, V.
The winning formula from this chain of brasseries (which includes Julien and Bofinger in Paris) is reproduced in Barcelona, with parlour palms and '20s posters; waiters with cloths draped over their arms and trays wielded at shoulder height. The house speciality is a huge platter of seafood, but the catholic range of dishes runs from carpaccio to ostrich. Puddings tend towards the Gallic; we can recommend the îles flottantes and the profiteroles. The set dinner menu at €21.80 is good value and includes wine.

Café de la Ribera

Plaça de les Olles 6, 08003 (93 319 50 72). Metro Barceloneta/14, 17, 40, 45, 51 bus. **Meals served** 11am-1am Tue-Thur; 11am-2am Fri, Sat. **Average** €. **Credit** DC, MC, V.

Though not as popular as it once was, between April and October this is still a peaceful place to sit out on the traffic-free square and watch the world walk by. For now, at least, for word is out that the pile of rubble opposite is to become a branch of Giorgio Armani. Dishes include peppers filled with cod or superb stuffed aubergines. The set lunch menu changes daily, and tapas are available all day.

Cal Pep ★

Plaça de les Olles 8, 08003 (93 310 79 61). Metro Barceloneta. **Meals served** 8pm-midnight Mon; 1.15-4pm, 8pm-midnight Tue-Sat. Closed Aug. **Average** €€. **Credit** AmEx, DC, MC, V.

Pep once left this great bar-restaurant to run the wonderful Passadis del Pep (*see p105*), but came back, missing the banter with his loyal customers. Most people choose to eat at the bar, but there's also a separate restaurant area consisting of a brick-lined room at the back decorated with a boar's head and antique cash registers. The fish and seafood dishes can be exceptional – the prawns are legendary and correspondingly pricey – and it pays to get here early.

Casa Delfín

Passeig del Born 36, 08003 (93 319 50 88). Metro Barceloneta. **Meals served** 7am-5pm Mon-Sat. Closed 3wks Aug. **Average** €. **Credit** AmEx, DC, MC, V.

For an impressive range of cheeses from all over Spain, and many other parts of Europe, try **Tot Formatge** (Passeig del Born 13).

Comerç 24

Alone among its neighbours, the Casa Delfin has resisted
the changes visited on the rest of the Born, now very much
an up-and-coming barri. While the beautiful people sun
themselves outside, inside is still a jovial workmen's
canteen, serving simple but tasty meat and fish at lunch
only. The extensive menú del dia is still good value, with
great sardines, fresh tuna and, during the season, roast
artichokes. Stews and soups are not quite as good, and
some of the salads tend to be overdressed. Those custardy
stalwarts flan and pudin are own-made and delicious.

La Cocotte

Passeig del Born 16, 08003 (93 319 17 34). Metro Jaume I. **Meals served** 1.30-4pm, 9pm-midnight Mon-Sat; 1.30-4pm Sun. **Average** €. **No credit cards**.

To style a restaurant around a 1950s casserole dish (cocotte) seems an odd conceit, but works rather well. Old *Good Housekeeping* ads vie for wall space with post-war tiling and Campbell's soup cans. The menu, unintentionally or not, harks forward a couple of decades to '70s exotica – chilli con carne, spring rolls, lasagne and moussaka. It's too postmodern for many tastes, but pretty good for these prices.

Comerç 24 ★

C/Comerç 24, 08003 (93 319 21 02). Metro Arc de Triomf. **Meals served** 1.30-4pm, 7.30pm-1am Mon-Fri; 7.30pm-1am Sat. Closed Aug. **Average** €€€. **Credit** AmEx, DC, MC, V.

Industrial chic – steel girders and jailhouse-grey paintwork punctuated with bursts of yellow and red – has surely just reached its apogee. Food is not so serious. The chef has created his own version of Ferran Adrià's famous tasting menu (*see p48*), playing with foams (asparagus is served with a warm grapefruit mousse) and deconstructing traditional favourites (DIY tortilla; just dip the ingredients into a warm egg yolk). A selection of tiny dishes roams the globe: tuna sashimi and seaweed on a wafer-thin pizza crust; Puy lentils with bacon and foie gras or squid stuffed with botifarra and anise. Waiters explain the provenance of every ingredient and encourage the ordering of the weird and wonderful, like a chocolate ganache served with bread, oil and salt. The real fun comes with coffee in a sachet full of chocolate-covered ginger Pop Rocks. Pour them on to your tongue and hold tight.

Coses de Menjar

Pla de Palau 7, 08003 (93 310 60 01). Metro Barceloneta or Jaume I. **Meals served** 1.30-4pm, 9-11.30pm Mon-Thur; 1.30-4pm, 9pm-midnight Fri, Sat. **Average** €€. **Credit** MC, V.

'Things to Eat' is yet another hit from the Parellada dining dynasty (others include Pla dels Àngels – *see p78* and Semproniana – *p136*), launched by daughter Ada. The decor is comfortable and luxurious, but livened up by Ada's trademark taste for quirkiness with wine glass chandeliers, menus glued to wine bottles and bent forks as napkin rings. Thoughtful and immaculately presented Mediterranean cooking – red mullet with almond sauce and fresh figs; pumpkin salad with soft cheese and cherries – plus a 300-strong wine list make it worth visiting, especially for lunch when the prices drop dramatically.

Mundial Bar

Espai Sucre ★

C/Princesa 53, 08003 (93 268 16 30). Metro Jaume I.
Meals served 9-11.30pm Tue-Sat. Closed Aug. **Average**
€€€. **Credit** MC, V.

In a neat reversal of everything your mother told you, the
only obligatory course in the 'Sugar Space' is pudding.
You choose between the three-course and the five-course
pudding menus, and only then decide whether to opt for
a small savoury dish; couscous with fried skate, perhaps,
or a lentil broth with grilled foie gras. The desserts
themselves are light and artfully constructed, using
combinations of sweet and savoury flavours to refreshing
effect. The sheer number of flavours in one dish – a soup
of shredded lychee holds a lozenge of ice-cream, infused
with apple, celery and eucalyptus and sprinkled with
ground cloves, among other things – can sometimes be a
little dizzying for the palate; the key is not to analyse the
parts, but enjoy the sum.

La Flauta Magica

C/Banys Vells 18, 08003 (93 268 46 94). Metro Jaume I.
Meals served 8.30-11.30pm Mon-Thur; 8.30pm-
midnight Fri, Sat; 8.30-11.30pm Sun. **Average** €€.
Credit DC, MC, V.

A hip hangout for New Age rich kids, with funky purple
and orange walls, Astor Piazzolla on the stereo and a
menu featuring inventive vegetarian dishes or organic
meat. The food looks divine (on the menu as well as the
plate), but the sauces for pasta and meat can be cloying.
Banana leaf tamales or sushi are a safer bet. A €1 cover
charge includes wholemeal bread and tapenade.

El Foro

C/Princesa 56, 08003 (93 310 10 20). Metro Arc de Triomf. **Meals served** 1-4pm, 9pm-midnight Tue-Thur; 1-4pm, 9pm-12.30am Fri-Sun. **Average** €€. **Credit** DC, MC, V.

This light and airy Argentine restaurant is ideal for combining vegetarians with baying carnivores, offering a range of salads (excellent), melted provolone (good), pizzas (fair) and pasta (average). The meat's the thing, you see: deliciously tender steaks cooked to perfection and full of flavour, as well as unusual cuts, and even chicken or duck. If you're feeling up to it, the mixed grill comes complete with its own miniature stove full of wood coals to keep it warm. The lunch menu is interesting, varied and very good value. Dodgy art exhibitions cover the walls, and downstairs there are occasional concerts and poetry readings.

Mundial Bar ★

Plaça Sant Agustí Vell 1, 08003 (93 319 90 56). Metro Arc de Triomf or Jaume I. **Meals served** 10am-11.30pm Tue-Sat; 11am-4pm Sun. **Average** €. **No credit cards.**

A welcome antidote to many of the fussy, touristy, seafood restaurants hereabouts, Mundial is a no-nonsense bar-restaurant run by three generations of an extremely welcoming family. Be warned that some of the fare on offer has seen the inside of a tin or a freezer, but the parrillada (€24 for two), a towering heap of grilled langoustines, prawns, clams, razor clams, octopus and more, is a fantastic bargain.

Passadís del Pep ★

*Pla del Palau 2, 08003 (93 310 10 21). Metro
Barcelona.* **Meals served** 1.30-3.30pm, 9-11.30pm
Mon-Sat. Closed 3wks Aug. **Average** €€€€. **Credit**
AmEx, DC, MC, V.

It says something about this restaurant that it is almost
impossible to find (follow the long corridor at the side of
La Caixa) and yet is full every night. A colourful, lively
place, it isn't in the least bit stuffy despite the high prices
and excellent food. There is no menu; waiters will bring
plate after plate of superb seafood, and will keep your
glass topped up with excellent cava. Only once will you
have to make a decision, on whether you would like a fish
dish – highly recommended but not cheap. The final bill
varies according to the market prices of the day, but if
you resist the glittering ranks of whiskies, you can expect
to pay around €70 a head, including cava.

La Ribera

El Pebre Blau ★

C/Banys Vells 21, 08003 (93 319 13 08). Metro Jaume I.
Meals served 8.30pm-midnight daily. **Average** €€.
Credit MC, V.

The Catalan Gothic arches of these old stables are given
a subtle, intimate look with soft lighting and a cascade
of colourful lightshades. A French-Moroccan menu
includes excellent lamb tajine and inventive duck dishes,
such as duck with plantains and Mexican *mole* sauce.
Puds are also delicious; try the goat's cheese in a tuile
basket with ginger marmalade. Service is, seemingly
without exception, young, attentive and charming, and
Edith Piaf provides the final touch.

Peps Bufet

C/Grunyi 5, 08003 (93 310 07 09). Metro Jaume I.
Meals served 8.30pm-1am Tue-Sat. Closed Aug.
Average €. **Credit** MC, V.

A buffet of good-quality, seriously Catalan dishes in a
17th-century merchant's house. Anna and Xavier are
extremely friendly and ready to explain any of the dishes,
including young rabbit in rosemary sauce, pig's trotters
and empedrat (salt cod salad), but there's very little for
strict vegetarians. House wine is a must-try Priorat at a
fraction of the normal price, and the desserts are a
memorable selection of chocolate mousses, eggy custards
and fruit salads.

A branch of
French-
Moroccan
restaurant **El
Pebre Blau**
(above) can
be found at
**L'Ou Com
Balla**,
C/Banys Vells
20 (93 310
5378).

Pla de la Garsa ★

C/Assaonadors 13, 08003 (93 315 24 13). Metro Jaume I.
Meals served 8pm-1am daily. **Average** €€. **Credit**
AmEx, MC, V.

A 16th-century stable and dairy converted into an
elegant restaurant, with marble-topped tables and a
wrought-iron spiral staircase leading up to another

secluded dining room. The strong suits here are high-quality cheeses from around Spain, pâtés and cold meats, as well as local specialities such as greixera menorquina (Menorcan leek tart). For a selection, along with samplers of dishes based on traditional recipes, some dating back to medieval times, there is a taster menu at €13 per person. Desserts are similarly based on local traditions, and vary according to the religious calendar. There are two selection platters to choose from, both easily big enough for two.

La Reina

C/Sant Antoni dels Sombrerers 3, 08003 (93 319 53 71). Metro Barceloneta or Jaume I. **Meals served** 8.30pm-midnight Mon-Thur; 8.30pm-1am Fri, Sat; 8.30pm-midnight Sun. **Average** €€. **Credit** MC, V.

It would seem red and black is the new black. La Reina's peculiar Dracula-chic sweeps on to the dark, narrow street by way of a crimson carpet and flickering candles, spooking passers-by. Toothsome pleasures inside include a tender duck magret with caramelised apples and a generous tuna steak with aubergine and black olives (both served rare, naturally). Desserts are similarly good and include a sublime chocolate tart with passion fruit cream. Tucked inside the entrance is a collection of mismatched armchairs, with magazines and a chess board, where helpful waiters will ply you with drinks before a table becomes free.

Restaurant L'Econòmic

Plaça Sant Agustí Vell 13, 08003 (93 319 64 94). Metro Arc de Triomf. **Meals served** 12.30-4.30pm Mon-Fri. Closed Aug. **Average** €. **No credit cards**.

L'Econòmic is a deep narrow restaurant lined with Andalucian tiles and the owner's oil paintings. It's always packed, but there are chairs on the pretty plaça outside for anyone waiting for a table. The set lunch offers old favourites such as escudella (stew), followed often by galtes de ternera (calves' cheek) or roast rabbit, and an unusually good range of puddings, including a dreamy lemon mousse.

Rodrigo

C/Argenteria 67, 08003 (93 310 30 20). Metro Jaume I. **Meals served** 8am-5pm, 8.30pm-1am Mon; 8am-5pm Tue; 8am-5pm, 8.30pm-1am Wed-Sun. **Average** €. **Credit** MC, V.

A bargain institution, famous for bocadillos, towering club sandwiches and vermouth. There are also full meals at lunchtime, featuring all the usual Catalan suspects. Things can get a little chaotic among the jumble of marble-topped tables, and this is emphatically not a place for an intimate meal à deux or anyone with a headache.

Pla de la Garsa. *See p105.*

Salero

Salero

C/Rec 60, 08003 (93 319 80 22). Metro Barceloneta.
Meals served 1.30-4pm, 9pm-midnight Mon-Wed;
1.30-4pm, 9pm-1am Thur, Fri; 9pm-1am Sat. Closed 2wks
Aug. **Average** €. **Credit** AmEx, MC, V.
A stylish, candlelit space where you can hear a
preponderance of English accents. The dishes come from
all corners of the globe – mee goreng, kangaroo steak,
lamb with rosemary – and are impressively presented,
but there are occasional triumphs of style over substance.
Cheesecake with marmalade may look and sound
interesting, but it tastes like, well, cheesecake with
marmalade. The music and atmosphere are cool and
relaxed, however, and apart from the cover charge, prices
are unfashionably low.

Santa Maria

*C/Comerç 17, 08003 (93 315 12 27). Metro Arc de
Triomf.* **Meals served** 1.30-3.30pm, 8.30pm-12.30am
Tue-Sat. Closed 3wks Aug. **Average** €€. **Credit** V.
Young acclaimed chef Paco Guzmán, another to learn his
art under Ferran Adrià (*see p48*), has been at the
vanguard of the new wave of designer tapa restaurants.
Not so much tapas as samplers, at Santa Maria you can
try a saucer of tuna mojama (thinly sliced and cured), or

Alongside Santa Maria del Mar, the smell of roasting nuts leads to **Casa Gispert** (C/Sombrerers 23) and huge baskets of almonds and hazelnuts fresh from the magnificent wood-burning oven.

a tiny bowl of perfectly al dente fried rice with chicken and vegetables. Most of the savoury offerings are well-executed international standards such as sushi and falafel, but the desserts are where things get really interesting. Try the pasión de Lola: a shot glass layered with Pop Rocks (all the rage this season), raspberries, a creamy passion fruit mousse and topped with a 'head' of dense beer foam; or the 'Dracula', where the children's favourite is dismantled and presented as raspberry and Coca-Cola mousses. With Pop Rocks, naturally.

Senyor Parellada

C/Argenteria 37, 08003 (93 310 50 94). Metro Jaume I.
Meals served 1-3.45pm, 8.30-11.45pm Mon-Sat.
Average €. **Credit** AmEx, DC, MC, V.
Senyor Parellada opened in autumn 2001 with a ritzier look and a new menu. The desperately old-fashioned concept of starters and main courses has been replaced with a system of various medium-sized platillos, which will arrive in stages (sound familiar?) and will comprise tasty Catalan favourites (plus ça change…). Try the seafood, or the ferociously good xai a les dotze cabeces d'all (lamb with 12 heads of garlic). Prices appear to have dropped a bit and, thankfully, the long-suffering, old-school waiters are still with us.

Sikkim

Sikkim

Plaça Comercial 1, 08003 (93 268 43 13). Metro Barceloneta or Jaume I. **Meals served** 9pm-1am Mon-Sat. **Average** €€. **Credit** MC, V.

Bordello lighting, wafting red chiffon and a generous scattering of bric-a-brac from India give this restaurant a cosy, intimate feel. Despite the decor, the food is mainly Mediterranean, mixing local ingredients with the occasional piece of exotica, such as shark or crocodile meat. Try the red mullet in shiitake oil with braised sweet potato, seared tuna with three-onion jam and lemon cream.

International

Bunga Raya

C/Assaonadors 7, 08003 (93 319 31 69). Metro Jaume I. **Meals served** 8pm-midnight Tue-Sun. **Average** €. **No credit cards**.

A narrow downstairs dining room has Malaysian tourist posters on the bamboo-lined walls, and often a Malaysian video as a soundtrack; the upstairs room is airy and peaceful. The great value set dinner involves beef rendang, chicken curry, lamb satay, squid and pickles, sambal and coconut, as well as a beer and a dessert. A friendly place, where service treads the line between relaxed and slow.

El Celler de Macondo

C/Consellers 4, 08003 (93 319 43 72). Metro Jaume I.
Meals served *Apr-Oct* 1pm-1am daily. *Nov-Mar* 6pm-1am Mon, Tue, Thur; 2pm-midnight Fri-Sun. **Average** €.
Credit AmEx, DC, MC, V.

Macondo was the name of the imaginary village in *One Hundred Years of Solitude*, fans of which will recognise myriad other references from the butterflies on the menus to the names of the dishes. Arnulfo, a charming Colombian, has bounced back from a legal wrangle with Garcia Marquez's representatives to create a little corner of his home country in the Born. Among other Colombian favourites, the speciality is 'arepizzas' – made with an arepa (a Latin American corn cake) base, and a variety of toppings. There's also a good wine list, with plenty of Chilean and Argentinian offerings.

Gente de Pasta

Passeig de Picasso 10, 08003 (93 268 70 17). Metro Ciutadella. **Meals served** 1-4pm, 2pm-12.30am daily.
Average €€. **Credit** DC, MC, V.

Depending on your point of view (or age, probably), Gente de Pasta is an innovative and funky place to munch on Italian classics while a DJ spins electronica lite, or it's a feeding trough for the under-30s. Some of the dishes work well – a caprese salad laden with anchovies and capers, or a risotto spiked with dill and pert little prawns – but the pasta dishes are a bit so-so; linguine with mushrooms was very oily, and spaghetti puttanesca a bit thin. The look is high ceilings, austere silver paint and dramatic spotlighting. It's rather like eating in a staff canteen while someone shines a torch on your head.

Habana Vieja

C/Banys Vells 2, 08002 (93 268 25 04). Metro Jaume I.
Meals served 10am-4pm, 8.30pm-midnight Mon-Thur; 8pm-1am Fri, Sat; 1pm-1am Sun. **Average** €€. **Credit** AmEx, DC, MC, V.

A funky and convivial Cuban restaurant with turquoise paintwork and, naturally, a great soundtrack. Like it says, this is a taste of old Havana; ropa vieja ('old rope' – a misleading term for what is actually very tender shredded beef, cooked with mild chillies) and arroz congri (rice with black beans) are complemented with authentic trimmings – machuquillos de Elleguá, fried balls of minced pork and plantain, are much better than they sound. For some really indulgent comfort food, finish your meal with the torrejas Habana Vieja: slices of bread dipped in egg and fried with cinnamon; and make sure you wash the whole thing down with plenty of Mojitos.

Since 1919, the Sans family has been importing and blending coffees from all around the world, as well as over 300 types of tea; try them at **El Magnífico** (C/Argenteria 64).

Down the pubs

The Philharmonic (C/Mallorca 204, 93 451 11 53) claims to be the only English pub in Barcelona that serves a full English breakfast at 9am. This claim remains untested, at least by us, as it's early afternoon before we swap the sunlight for its enormous back room. On our way in we pass a stag party starting the day with pints and football at the bar. Breakfast is everything it should be and we scan the programme that keeps the pub busy all week: tango and line-dancing, a pub quiz on Thursdays, and live music leaning towards jazz and blues.

Barcelona pubs vie with each other for the patronage of the homesick expat in need of Sky Sports, draught beer and general knowledge questions. With this in mind, we head down to another community-oriented English pub, **The Black Horse** (C/Allada-Vermell 16, 93 268 33 38), that holds its bilingual quiz on Sundays. Outside, local kids are kicking a ball around, while inside, it's

a packed house for the Six Nations. We settle down under a low arched ceiling in one of its four pleasantly poky little rooms for pints of John Smith's and Boddingtons.

Heading back towards Via Laietana we stick our heads round the door at **The Clansman** (C/Vigatans 13, 93 319 71 69), tempted by the prospect of Gillespie's Scottish Stout. Instead we forge on to our first Irish pub of the day, **The Shamrock** (C/Tallers 72, 93 412 46 36), on the other side of La Rambla. With plenty of green paint, pool, darts, table football and big-screen sports, it's unpretentious and popular with expatriate tradespeople filling Barcelona's skills gap.

Towards the sea and off La Rambla, **The Quiet Man** (C/Marquès de Barberà 11, 93 412 12 19) is one place that's aimed at a mainly Catalan crowd: it has no TV and a beer menu with German and Belgian bottled lagers. Wooden booths divide the bar area into semi-private little alcoves, there's a three-piece band crammed on to a tiny stage, and students playing party games in the back room.

After that, it's a long metro ride across to the **Michael Collins** (Plaça Sagrada Família 4, 93 459 19 64): a gamble, as it's out on its own, but it pays off. There's a band somewhere at the bottom end of this extended U, hidden behind the smoke and all but drowned out by the hubbub. The enamelled tin Guinness ads and imported porcelain knick-knacks have worked their magic, and Americans, Brits and locals are all talking nineteen to the dozen. As we leave we exchange sympathetic glances with the glassy-eyed stuffed duck in the case by the door, and getting into the taxi realise that our brief instructions to the driver are the first Spanish we've spoken all day.

Little Italy

C/Rec 30, 08003 (93 319 79 73). Metro Jaume I. **Meals served** 1.30-4pm Mon-Sat; 8pm-midnight Mon-Thur; 8pm-12.30am Fri, Sat. Closed 2wks Aug. **Average** €€. **Credit** AmEx, DC, MC, V.

Apart from a short list of pasta and risotto primi, this is not so much Little Italy as Little Mediterranean, with an emphasis on good, fresh market produce. This is also one of the few places in town to make a decent salad and serve your main course with vegetables. Its split-level, candlelit dining room and, above all, its jazz – musicians on Wednesday and Thursday or Ella, Louis and friends the rest of the week – attract a slightly older, diverse crowd.

Al Passatore

Pla del Palau 8, 08003 (93 319 78 51). Metro Barceloneta. **Meals served** 1pm-12.30am Mon-Wed; 1pm-1am Thur-Sun. **Average** €. **Credit** MC, V.

There's a good range of pasta dishes and a decent-value set lunch, but the fabulous pizzas, piping hot from the wood-fired oven, are the real reason to come here. The restaurant's enormous popularity means that service gets a bit pushed, and there is usually a queue. Get there earlier to grab one of the outside tables on the square.

Taira

C/Comerç 7, 08003 (93 310 24 97). Metro Arc de Triomf. **Meals served** 1-4pm, 9pm-12.30am Tue-Sun. **Average** €€. **Credit** AmEx, DC, MC, V.

Taira's giant plate-glass windows frame an elaborate concoction of hi-design woodwork and projections, all ablaze with candlelight. Fashion foibles, such as the uncomfortable but oh-so-hip seating, are more than made

Wood-fired pizzas are the highlight of Italian restaurant **Al Passatore** *(left)* and its two branches **Al Passatore**, Moll de Gregal 25 (93 225 0047) and **Montello**, Via Laietana 42, 08003 (93 310 3526).

The best winetasting

La Barcelonina de Vins i Esperits
See p143.

Cata 1.81
See p131.

Quimet i Quimet
See p202.

Va de Vi
See p125.

La Vinya del Senyor
See p126.

Teranga

up for by the food, which you can also take away. It is
swiftly prepared in the open kitchen bar and includes
clean-tasting crunchy salads, delicate soups, and an
elegantly presented range of very affordable sushi and
sashimi. The real strength here, though, is the noodle and
wok dishes: gomoku yakisoba ebi is a treat not to be
missed. And the desserts? As Japanese as apple pie.

Teranga

C/Nau 9, 08003 (93 310 33 65). Metro Jaume I. **Meals
served** 1-5pm, 8.30pm-1am Mon, Wed-Sun. **Average** €.
No credit cards.
Serving simple Senegalese food in a one-time Castilian
mesón, Teranga has a certain, low-key charm, attracting
a mix of young Catalans and Senegalese from the
neighbourhood. The food is somewhat variable; spicy
spinach on a bed of sweet potato is delicious, as is the
ginger and pineapple juice, but dumplings are bland, and
the lamb stew heavy and uninspiring. In summer there are
tables out on the unexciting but quiet square, away from
the main Born rat run. Plans are also afoot to make an
entrance facing C/Argenteria. Temporary exhibitions and
weekly concerts (not necessarily Senegalese) are also held.

Euskal Extea. *See p 118.*

Vegetarian

Comme Bio

Via Laietana 28, 08003 (93 319 89 68/www.commebio.es).
Metro Jaume I. **Meals served** 1-4pm, 8.30-11pm Mon-Fri;
1-4pm, 8.30-midnight Sat; 1-4pm, 8.30-11pm Sun.
Average €. Credit AmEx, DC, MC, V.

The Comme Bio chain has become a lifesaver for
vegetarians all over Spain, and this stylish branch always
has queues at lunchtime for the downstairs all-you-can-
eat bargain buffet of soups, salads and pastas. Upstairs,
there's partial waiter service and a choice of slightly more
complex dishes, such as wild mushroom ragoût or
spinach and ricotta pancakes, plus a well-stocked organic
food shop.

Cafés & Bars

Bass Bar

*C/Assaonadors 25, 08003 (no phone). Metro Jaume I/17,
19, 40, 45, N8 bus.* **Open** 8pm-3am Mon-Fri; 9.30pm-3am
Sat, Sun. **No credit cards**.

A couple of battered sofas, a pile of free music rags, and
a handful of locals working on their dreadlocks jostle for
space in this small offbeat bar. Exhibitions of local artists
and collectives adorn the walls, and the music covers
everything from Spanish ska to world drumming to Latin.

Café del Born

*Plaça Comercial 10, 08003 (93 268 32 72). Metro Jaume
I.* **Open** 9am-1am Mon-Wed; 9am-3am Thur-Sat; 9am-1am
Sun. **Credit** MC, V.

Among the first cafés to herald this area's stylish
renaissance some years ago, the airy Café del Born now
puts on flamenco on Mondays, cool jazz on Tuesdays and
poetry reading on Wednesdays. Light snacks are
available, including a weekend brunch, veggie options
and delicious cakes. From the tables outside, you can
watch the city's finest library slowly emerge from the
skeletal wreck of the old Born market.

La Estrella de Plata

*Pla del Palau 9, 08003 (93 319 60 07). Metro
Barceloneta.* **Open** 1-4pm, 8pm-midnight Mon-Sat.
No credit cards.

Time was when La Estrella's reputation for world-class
tapas attracted aficionados from far and wide. Today the
following is limited to those that can still afford it:
uptowners – witness the serried ranks of Audis – and a
babel of Eurotrash. While the tapas (with a few notable

Be sure to
pick up the
latest wine
catalogue at
the well-
stocked
Vila Viniteca
(C/Agullers
7-9).
Beautifully
designed, they
have become
collectors'
items.

L'Hivernacle

such as artichoke hearts stuffed with quails' eggs) have lost
their edge, the prices have made healthy progress. Check
your bank balance before ordering the seafood.

Euskal Extea

*Placeta Montcada 1-3, 08003 (93 310 21 85). Metro
Jaume I.* **Open** *Bar* 9am-11.30pm Tue-Sat; 12.45-3.30pm
Sun. *Restaurant* 1-3.30pm, 9-11.30pm Tue-Sat. Closed
Aug. **Credit** MC, V.
This Basque cultural centre is the granddaddy of pintxo
bars hereabouts and embodies its region's reputation
for culinary excellence. Platters laden with dainty
morsels from sublime hake mousse to botifarra with
cabrales cheese appear on the bar at about midday and
7pm. The restaurant at the back is a superb place to
sample more substantial Basque fare, and does a great
lunch menu for €9.

Glüh Bar

*C/Verdaguer i Callís 6, 08003 (93 310 64 00). Metro
Urquinaona.* **Open** 8pm-3am Tue-Sat. **Meals served**
9pm-1am Tue-Sat. Closed 2wks Aug. **Credit** AmEx,
MC, V.
Down one of the narrowest streets of sleepy Sant Pere,
this tiny bar has something of the beach bar about it.
The scene is set by a mixture of chunky wooden fittings,

rich colours and a giant painting of jamming musicians.
Most nights there is a storytelling session or a band –
generally Brazilian or Cuban – and fusion dishes (the
likes of horse carpaccio 'Japanese-style') are served up
on the mezzanine.

L'Hivernacle

*Parc de la Ciutadella, 08003 (93 295 40 17). Metro Arc
de Triomf.* **Open** 10am-1am daily. **Credit** AmEx, DC,
MC, V.
An elegant and luminous bar inside the beautiful iron-
and-glass hivernacle (greenhouse) of the Parc de la
Ciutadella, built in 1884. With three parts (one shaded
room, one unshaded and a terrace), Bar Hivernacle hosts
exhibitions and occasional jazz and classical concerts. As
well as the plants around the bar, there's a fine display
of tropical greenery in one of the rooms alongside.

La Idea

*Plaça Comercial 2, 08003 (93 268 87 87/
www.ideaborn.com). Metro Jaume I.* **Open** 8am-1am
Mon-Thur; 8am-3am Fri; 10am-3am Sat; 10am-11pm Sun.
No credit cards.
Spacious and with a comfortable sitting-room feel, La Idea
has a small, eclectic selection of books for sale, more than
a dozen international newspapers and plenty of computers

La Idea. *See p119.*

located downstairs (€1.20 per half-hour). In the main room, a massive floor-to-ceiling canvas bears the UN Universal Declaration of Human Rights, and the café often has exhibitions focusing on human rights issues.

Local.bar

C/Ases 7 (Plaça Fossar de les Moreres), 08003 (93 319 13 57). Metro Jaume I. **Open** 1pm-3am daily. **No credit cards**.
The Local.bar has two entrances; the first, from Plaça Fossar de les Moreres, leads into a small space which occasionally becomes a dance floor on animated nights. The other entrance leads into a peaceful space decorated with local artists' work. It's a great bet for a late drink when all around is closed. What's more, the bar also allows you free Internet access when you buy a drink.

Miramelindo

Passeig del Born 15, 08003 (93 310 37 27). Metro Jaume I. **Open** 8pm-2.30am Mon-Sat; 7pm-2.30am Sun. **No credit cards**.
A classic of the Born neighbourhood, Miramelindo is so well established it can almost dispense with signs outside. Inside, it glows with the mellow sheen of surfaces on which care is unstintingly lavished every day. Everything from the spotless mirror to the tiled corner, where grave-faced cocktail waiters in long aprons prepare Mojitos, exudes class.

Local.bar. *See p121*.

La Morera

Plaça Fossar de les Moreres 5, 08003 (617 810 312).
Metro Jaume I. **Open** 5pm-midnight Tue, Wed;
5pm-1.30am Thur; 6pm-2.30am Fri-Sun.
No credit cards.

A more popular recent addition than the 'Eternal Flame'
(to remember the martyrs of 1714) that lights the other
side of the square, this cosy llesqueria has a vaguely
Moroccan feel, with deep pink walls, candles and low
tables and stools. The choice of wines is impressive and
panes of glass set into the floor provide a window into a
larger room below.

Mudanzas

C/Vidrieria 15, 08003 (93 319 11 37). Metro Jaume I.
Open 10am-2.30am daily. **Credit** MC, V.

Few of the many cafés and bars surrounding the
increasingly trendy Born area manage to capture the
relaxed ambience of this bar, with its chequered tiled floor
and marble-topped tables. There's a rack of newspapers
and magazines, many in English, and some tables outside.

El Nus

C/Mirallers 5, 08003 (93 319 53 55). Metro Jaume I. **Open**
7.30pm-2.30am Mon, Tue, Thur-Sun. **No credit cards**.

White lace curtains, stone walls, dusty chandeliers, wood and the liberal use of red paint make this a charming place to enjoy a quiet drink, while low-key jazz plays in the background. The sage-looking gent in the large black and white photo fixed to the ceiling is the bar's original owner.

Palau Dalmases

C/Montcada 20, 08003 (93 310 06 73). Metro Jaume I.
Open 8pm-2am Tue-Sat; 6-10pm Sun. **Credit** MC, V.
An elderly gentleman greets customers at the door of this 17th-century residence, and ushers them through the courtyard to the 'Espai Barroc'. The walls are adorned with paintings, there is ornate furniture, and spectacular displays of flowers, fruit and aromatic herbs give it the look of an Italian still life. Suitably baroque music plays. It's deeply eccentric, decadent and a tad pretentious, but soothing to ear, nose and eye – and worth the high prices.

Ribborn

C/Antic de Sant Joan 3, 08003 (93 310 71 48).
Metro Jaume 1. **Open** 8pm-3am daily. **Credit** MC, V.
The perfect palliative for the Born's airs, Ribborn is noisy, lively and unpretentious. Locals, bathed in a dim red glow, shout above the likes of James Brown or some live sounds. The staff mix a fine cocktail and there is Guinness on tap.

To stock up on ham, cheese and bread for a picnic in nearby Parc de la Ciutadella, visit the **Mercat Santa Caterina** on Passeig Lluís Companys.

A round-up of drinks

NON-ALCOHOLIC

The three basic types of coffee are café solo (cafè sol in Catalan), a small strong black coffee; cortado/tallat, the same but with a little milk; and café con leche/cafè amb llet, a white coffee, but with more milk and less water than in northern Europe or America. Then there's café americano (a large white coffee diluted with more water), and spiked coffee: a carajillo, which is a short, black coffee with a liberal dash of brandy. If you want another type of drink, you have to specify, such as carajillo de ron (rum) or carajillo de whisky. A trifàsico is a carajillo with a bit of milk. Decaffeinated coffee (descafeinado) is widely available, but ask for it de màquina if you don't want a sachet of Nescafé with hot milk. For advice on ordering tea, *see* p167 **Taking the strain**.

Freshly squeezed orange juice is surprisingly uncommon and is often served here as dessert, while horchata (tiger nut milk) makes a unique and refreshing drink in summer. Still water is agua sin gas and sparkling is agua con gas. Water is often served at room temperature (natural) unless you ask for it chilled (fria).

BEER

The most common brand of beer in Catalonia is Damm, with Estrella – a strong lager – the most popular variety. Damm also produces an even stronger lager (Voll Damm) and a dark one (Bock Damm). For draught beer, ask for it de barril. A caña is around half a (UK) pint, a quinto smaller still. Occasionally, you will find jarras, which are more like a pint.

SPIRITS

Best known are the full-bodied, dark brandies, such as Torres 5 or 10, which have been aged five or ten years respectively. Mascaró, Magno and Carlos III are also well worthing trying. Anís is popular, as is a range of very strong firewaters, including orujo and absinthe (absenta). Galician orujo is similar to French eau de vie or Italian grappa. It is distilled from what is left after wine grapes have been pressed and is a good digestive.

s:pic

C/Ribera 10, 08003 (93 310 15 95). Metro Barceloneta.
Open 9pm-2.30am Mon-Thur; 9pm-3am Fri, Sat. **Credit** MC, V.

From the name on down, s:pic sticks to its 'more is more' principles and has roped in every element of trendoid bar design: glass floors, reflective ceilings, and an outbreak of plastic-furring. Its most stylish customers preen themselves in the diffused orange lighting and check out the competition, but ordinary punters are made welcome.

Suau

*Passeig del Born 30, 08003 (93 310 63 54). Metro
Barceloneta or Jaume I.* **Open** 3pm-3am Mon-Fri; 7pm-
3am Sat; 4.30pm-3am Sun. **No credit cards**.

The locals' powerful lobby for undisturbed sleep means
that Suau's outside terrace (along with all the others
hereabouts) has to be cleared as the witching hour
approaches. If downstairs, with garish Tutankhamen
mural, becomes too cramped, there's another – usually
empty – room upstairs. Tarot reading and imported beers
(among them Leffe and Chimay) are available.

Tèxtil Cafè

*C/Montcada 12-14, 08003 (93 268 25 98). Metro Jaume
I.* **Open** 10am-midnight Tue-Sun. **Credit** MC, V.

In the courtyard of the graceful 14th-century palace that
now houses the textile and Barbier-Mueller museums is
this peaceful oasis; an elegant place for a coffee in the
shade (or under gas heaters in winter), with decent
breakfast and lunch menus. The array of newspapers
improves the lot of anyone waiting to get served, which
can take forever.

La Tinaja

C/Esparteria 9, 08003 (93 310 22 50). Metro Jaume I.
Open 6pm-2am Mon-Sat. **Credit** AmEx, DC, MC, V.

The old crocks hanging like swallows' nests from the
beams, the collection of wrought-iron implements and the
lofty stone arches create an appealing rus in urbe
atmosphere – a near perfect spot to sample the standard
llesqueria menu, along with a good-value bottle of wine.
Finish off with the fine tarta de Santiago: almond cake on
to which you pour the accompanying glass of moscatell.

Txirimiri

C/Princesa 11, 08003 (93 310 18 05). Metro Jaume I.
Open noon-midnight Tue-Sun. Closed 1st 2wks Sept.
Credit MC, V.

Pintxo heaven would be a big airy place, where the
excellent Basque tapas would be free, you'd always get a
seat and the relaxed staff would welcome you with radiant
smiles. Perhaps there would also be occasional visits from
a Zeppo-like jester to twist balloons and perform magic
tricks. Alas, they still make you pay at Txirimiri.

Va de Vi

C/Banys Vells 16, 08003 (93 319 29 00). Metro Jaume I.
Open 6pm-1am Mon-Wed, Sun; 6pm-2am Thur; 6pm-3am
Fri, Sat. **Credit** MC, V.

Run by an artist who has a taste for wine and an eye for
Gothic extravagance, Va de Vi, with its 16th-century
arches, candles and heavy drapery, mixes atmospheric
sophistication with relaxed informality. The wine list

El Nus. *See p122.*

includes numerous unusual bottles, many of which are
available in a small tasting measure (cata), and the
llesqueria fare maintains the high standard.

La Vinya del Senyor

*Plaça Santa Maria 5, 08003 (93 310 33 79). Metro
Jaume I.* **Open** noon-1.30am Tue-Sat; noon-4pm Sun.
Credit DC, MC, V.
An elegant little wine-taster's bar with tables outdoors
from which to contemplate the majestic façade of Santa
Maria del Mar. With a superb list of more than 300 wines
and selected cavas, sherries and moscatells, changed
every 15 days, the Iberian ham and French cheese come
in very handy for their qualities of absorption.

El Xampanyet

C/Montcada 22, 08003 (93 319 70 03). Metro Jaume I.
Open noon-4pm, 6.30-11.30pm Tue-Sat; noon-4pm Sun.
Closed Aug. **Credit** MC, V.
Run by the same family since the 1930s, this 'little
champagne bar' is one of the eternal attractions on this
ancient street. It's lined with coloured tiles, barrels and
antique curios, and there are a few marble tables. The bar
has three specialities: anchovies, cider and 'champagne' (a
pretty plain cava, but very refreshing).

Eixample

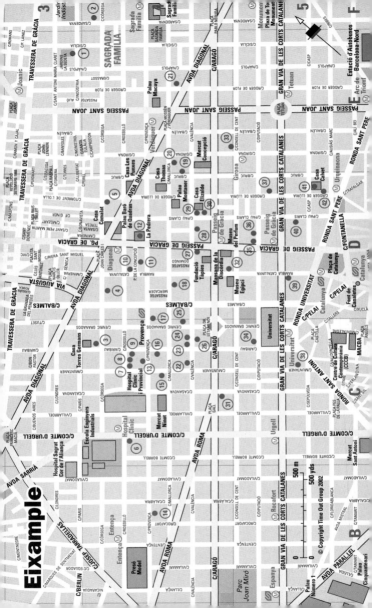

Restaurants

Alboroque

C/Mallorca 304, 08037 (93 458 08 55). Metro Verdaguer.
Meals served 1-4pm Mon-Wed; 1-4pm, 8-11.30pm Thur-Sat. Closed Aug. **Average** €. **Credit** MC, V.

Through a modest yellow-framed doorway, the blissfully restful Alboroque offers some of the best food in this price range, along with classical music, tasteful decor and immaculate service from an all-girl team. The cooking is light and fresh, with starters such as camembert croquettes, or Popeye salad of spinach and mushrooms. Main courses include interesting combinations such as sea bass a la vinagreta with beetroot, or rabbit in red wine. Alongside a cheeseboard and traditional favourites like sausage, there's a range of carpaccios and high-quality pasta dishes – al dente ruccula ravioli in a creamy walnut sauce is particularly good. Memorable desserts include brochette of fresh fruit with hot chocolate sauce.

El Asador de Burgos

C/Bruc 118, 08009 (93 207 31 60). Metro Verdaguer.
Meals served 1-4pm, 9-11pm Mon-Sat. Closed Aug.
Average €€€. **Credit** AmEx, DC, MC, V.

No messing around with design, vegetables or other trifles: this is solid Castilian food in a down-to-earth setting, with combinations of Jabugo ham, kidneys, sausages and so on. The main event is the 'asador', the large, wood-fired oven in which racks of lamb and whole suckling pigs are roasted to perfection. You'll need to book at least three hours in advance, especially mid-week, but it's worth it. The suckling pig is divine, with sweet, crispy skin and delicious tender flesh. The wine list is steep in price, but the house wine is reasonable and excellent value.

Casa Calvet ★

C/Casp 48, 08010 (93 412 40 12). Metro Urquinaona.
Meals served 1-3.30pm, 8.30-11pm Mon-Sat. **Average** €€€. **Credit** AmEx, DC, MC, V.

A criticism often levelled at the Modernistas was that of 'fachadisme' – a tendency to neglect the interior of a building behind a dazzling façade. Not so in Gaudí's Casa Calvet; the ground floor, where the elegant restaurant is situated, is full of glorious detail in the carpentry, stained glass and tiles. The food is also a delight; modern Catalan dishes of note include pea soup with little chunks of squid, succulent pigeon with Szechuan pepper and roast fennel, and tasty lamb 'meatballs' with creamy risotto. Puddings are supremely good – order the crunchy pine nut tart with foamed crema catalana at the beginning – and the wine list encyclopaedic.

Eixample

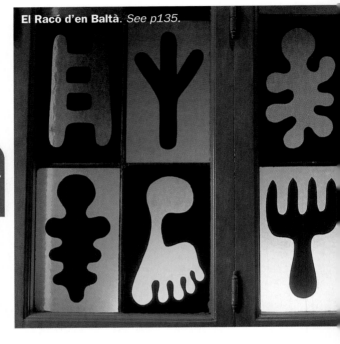

El Racó d'en Baltà. *See p135.*

Castro ★

C/Casanova 85, 08011 (93 323 67 84). Metro Urgell.
Meals served 1-4pm, 9pm-midnight Mon-Fri; 9pm-
midnight Sat. **Average** €€. **Credit** MC, V.

With industrial design, subtle lighting and ambient
house played at civilised levels, Castro has great
atmosphere, making it an ideal venue for a date. The
clientele is very varied in terms of age, orientation and
image-consciousness, and the food is largely excellent:
Mediterranean meat and fish cooked – in most instances
– with flair and imagination, though some dishes can
be a pinch oversalted and a fraction overcooked. Beef
carpaccio was a melting rendition, almost sweet in
flavour, and crowned with swathe upon swathe of
parmesan. A dish of wild mushrooms with prawns
proved also a good bet. Duck comes slathered in rich
fruits of the forest, and is delicious, as is the baked John
Dory and apple 'grumble'.

Ramón
Casas'
magnificent
modernista
tiling is not
the only thing
to look out for
at **Queviures
Murrià**
(C/Roger de
Llúria 85); the
cheeses are
outstanding,
as is the
selection of
wine.

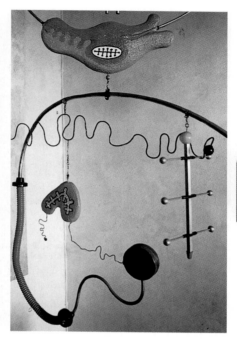

Cata 1.81

C/Valencia 181, 08011 (93 323 68 18). Metro Hospital Clínic or Passeig de Gràcia. **Meals served** 6pm-midnight Mon-Thur; 6pm-1am Fri, Sat. Closed last 3wks Aug. **Average €. Credit** AmEx, DC, MC, V.

'Cata' is Catalan for tasting, and is the raison d'être of this bright and slightly austere little place. Oenophiles flock to sample 25cl decanters of whatever takes their fancy from the impressive and wide-ranging wine list, while the platillos (little dishes) to go with it hit a different spot. Not so much dishes as saucerfuls, the adventurous menu includes mini hamburgers with tiny cones of chips, salted foie with strawberry sauce and miniature parcels of cheese and tomato; competent, fun even, but overshadowed by soft, treacly pigs' trotters with figs, walnuts and honey ice-cream. Cata is very popular with Catalan gastronomic luminaries, who, sadly, get the best of the service.

Fuse

*C/Roger de Llúria 40, 08009 (93 301 74 99). Metro
Passeig de Gràcia.* **Meals served** 1-4pm, 9pm-midnight
Mon-Fri; 9pm-midnight Sat. **Average** €. **Credit** AmEx,
DC, MC, V.
'A laboratory of the sensations' – that means they lay on
the grub before carting off the tables and wheeling in the
DJ, as at any parish hall disco. As with all of these
restaurant-clubs, the menu is fashionably globetrotting:
as well as the usual exotica – chicken yakitori, four-cheese
panzerotti and Thai fish curry – there is a monthly
changing set menu offering dishes from a certain country.
Our visit coincided with Tibet month; the scene was
nicely set with Tibetan wall-hangings and slide
projections, but inevitably the menu promised much more
than it could deliver. It's fun, though, and a friendly place
with chilled music. Go with a bunch of friends, and don't
order too ambitiously.

Jaume de Provença

C/Provença 88, 08029 (93 430 00 29). Metro Entença.
Meals served 1-4pm, 9-11.30pm Tue-Sat; 1-4pm Sun.
Closed Aug. **Average** €€€. **Credit** AmEx, DC, MC, V.
Jaume de Provença opened in 1981, the era of the parsley
garnish, the crêpe suzette and the decorative stein, and
little has changed here since, with piped Glenn Miller in
the lavatories and generous sized portions (remember
those?). It's reasonably smart but comfortable, with food
to match – wild mushrooms and prawns with pine nut
dressing comes with boiled carrots and french beans,
and a request for a steak cooked rare meets with a

Long-running
Gràcia
institution **El
Glop** *p160*
has a branch
at **El Glop de
la Rambla**
Rambla
Catalunya 65
(93 487
0097).

Semproniana. *See p137.*

furrowed brow from the waiter, concerned about your delicate foreign palate. There is an attractive wine list, albeit with some bottles quite steeply marked up.

Jordi Vilà

C/Indústria 69, 08025 (617 78 05 32). Metro Sagrada Família. **Meals served** 1.30-3pm, 9-11pm Mon-Fri; 9-11pm Sat. Closed 2wks Aug. **Average** €€€. **Credit** AmEx, DC, MC, V.

Jordi Vilà has now taken his finetuned cooking to a new uptown location after getting his start at El Abrevadero in Poble Sec. The brand new decor, wine cellar and richly diverse menu make this a restaurant on the rise. Ordering à la carte opens the door to highly creative collages of taste and colour spun off from Catalan and Provençal standards. How about a salad of luxury lettuces, beetroot purée and warm sliced squid? Main courses announcing wild rice, game fowl or baked fish always surprise with unexpected combinations and flavours. A great way to explore is the gourmet menu, with four savoury courses and a couple of desserts.

La Provença

C/ Provença 242, 08008 (93 323 23 67). Metro Diagonal.
Meals served 1.30-3.30pm, 9-11.30pm daily. **Average** €€.
Credit AmEx, DC, MC, V.

One of a chain of French restaurants, La Provença looks good, feels good; and some of it tastes good. Starters and desserts are more successful than main courses, which tend to take a sludgy approach to sauce-making. A sea urchin au gratin starter was rich and soupy, and poached eggs 'à la Périgordine' were good, too, offset with a rich meat jus. Unfortunately, the same jus featured heavily with the sea bass main course, to its detriment. Desserts are much more interesting, but in general this is a place for families or business meetings, with good-value set menus for groups.

El Racó d'en Baltà

C/Aribau 125, 08036 (93 453 10 44). FCG Provença/ Metro Diagonal. **Meals served** 1-4pm, 9-11pm Tue-Sat. Closed 3wks Aug. **Average** €€. **Credit** MC, V.

This two-storey restaurant with a bar next door offers modern Catalan cuisine in original and vibrant surroundings. The best seats are in the airy upstairs room, where you can enjoy spring lamb in a reduction of brandy and honey, or a herbed goat's cheese salad, followed by a delicious banana bavarois trickled with golden syrup. El Racó d'en Baltà's decor is a bizarre mix of '50s memorabilia (menus are presented on old record sleeves) and artist Steve Forster's sculptures incorporating spray-painted Marigolds and bathplugs. The clientele is generally young and up for it, and the service very friendly and informal.

El Rodizio

C/Consell de Cent 403, 08009 (93 265 51 12). Metro Girona. **Meals served** 1-4pm, 8.30pm-midnight Mon-Thur; 1-4pm, 8.30pm-1am Fri, Sat; 1-4pm Sun. **Average** €. **Credit** MC, V.

Loosely based on a Brazilian rodizio – where huge skewers of meat are carved at your table until you beg them to stop – the only difference here is that you help yourself. Every sort of meat turns slowly under a grill – just point at what you want, then help yourself to the fantastic range of salads and vegetables, not to mention all the Catalan trimmings: pa amb tomàquet, several types of olive oil and even a huge pan of paella. A drink, coffee, cheese and pudding are included in the price: a staggeringly low €7.75 at lunchtime or a slightly higher €11.50 at night.

Sar Gan Tan A

C/Enric Granados 34, 08008 (93 451 45 03). Metro Liceu. **Meals served** 1-3.45pm, 9-11.45pm daily. **Average** €. **Credit** MC, V.

Les Quinze Nits *p39* offers modern Catalan dishes at rock-bottom prices as do its three Eixample branches: **L'Hostal de Rita** C/Aragó 279 (93 487 2376); **El Palauet Luca** C/Enric Granados 23 (93 323 1635); **La Polpa** C/Enric Granados 69 (93 323 8308).

Eixample

Entering Sar Gan Tan A is a bit like fighting your way through an overgrown jungle: tendrils, leaves and bushes sprout from every surface. The fixed menu is excellent value, with modern Catalan favourites such as leek tart, seafood vol-au-vents and brochette of tiger prawn and salmon. There's also an appropriately leafy range of salads and some imaginative desserts.

Semproniana

C/Rosselló 148, 08036 (93 453 18 20). Metro Hospital Clínic. **Meals served** 1.30-4pm, 9-11.30pm Mon-Thur; 1.30-4pm, 9pm-midnight Fri, Sat. **Average** €€. **Credit** AmEx, DC, MC, V.

From the same stable as Pla dels Àngels and Coses de Menjar in the Born and very much in the same vein, Semproniana is a colourfully painted wonderland of floaty gauze drapes, twigs glittering with glass pendants, dusty ancient books, and coat hooks and napkin rings made from contorted cutlery. The wording of the menu is suitably capricious; roast pigeon becomes 'the bird which flies on the ground', and a dense chocolate mousse becomes 'delirium tremens'. The food, which might include a creamy courgette soup or a hunk of cod with calçots, is not bad, but rarely a match for the atmosphere.

Tragaluz ★

Passatge de la Concepció 5, 08008 (93 487 01 96). Metro Diagonal. **Meals served** 1.30-4pm, 8.30pm-midnight Mon-Wed, Sun; 1.30-4pm, 8.30pm-1am Thur-Sat. **Average** €€€. **Credit** AmEx, DC, MC, V.

The first thing anyone will tell you about Tragaluz is that its glorious, light-filled interior was designed by '80s wunderkind Javier Mariscal; in fact, he only designed the menus. The next thing about which they'll wax lyrical is the food, and here they're not wrong. How about a delicious warm duck salad to start, or a creamy cauliflower soup with lychee granita and jamón iberico, followed by tender, flaky sea bass with an onion millefeuille and tomato marmalade? Puddings are spectacularly good; try apricot and strawberry soup with iced yoghurt and Szechuan pepper. Downstairs, Tragarrapid serves lighter meals all day, and the group also runs a Japanese restaurant across the street.

La Tramoia

Rambla de Catalunya 15, 08007 (93 412 36 34). Metro Passeig de Gràcia. **Meals served** 12.30pm-1.30am daily. **Average** €. **Credit** AmEx, DC, MC, V.

Of the various chains of theme restaurants and tapas megabars that monopolise the city centre, particularly Passeig de Gràcia, La Tramoia is unusual in offering decent food to go with its marketing/design concept. Downstairs there's a wide range of hot and cold tapas,

Irresistible handmade chocolate of every conceivable type and in every conceivable shape awaits at **Cacao Sampaka** (C/Consell de Cent 292).

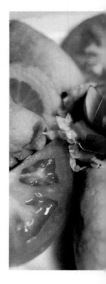

Eixample

while upstairs the light but tight restaurant has more substantial Mediterranean food, including various vegetable and meat dishes grilled on the barbecue you pass as you enter. Daily specials might include a delicious lentil, mushroom and seafood risotto or succulent hamburgers with foie (and certainly no bun). The desserts are competent crowd-pleasers.

Windsor

C/Còrsega 286, 08004 (93 415 84 83). Metro Diagonal.
Meals served 1-4pm, 8.30-11pm Mon-Fri; 8.30-11pm Sat. Closed Aug. **Average** €€€. **Credit** AmEx, DC, MC, V.
Depending on what you look for in a foreign dining experience, your heart can sink on entering a restaurant full of Brits and Americans, where English is the lingua franca. Have courage. The dishes on offer here are unreconstructed Catalan, consummately executed and wholly dependent on what's in season, from artichoke soup with cod mousse to venison cannelloni with black truffle sauce. The list of puddings, each accompanied by different suggestions for dessert wines, is a real highlight. La Selva Negra is a triumphant paean to current vogues – black forest gâteau presented as stacked slabs of chocolate cake next to swirls of cherry sorbet and vanilla cream foam. Very postmodern. Very good.

Al Diwan.
See p139.

Eixample

La Yaya Amelia

C/Sardenya 364, 08025 (93 456 45 73). Metro Sagrada Familia. **Meals served** 1pm-midnight Mon-Sat. Closed 2wks Aug. **Average** €€. **Credit** AmEx, DC, MC, V.

'Grandma Amelia' is just a couple of blocks behind the Sagrada Familia in an otherwise gastronomically forsaken part of the city. It doesn't look like much – overlit and cheaply furnished – but once inside aperitifs are offered, a fabulous wine list is knowledgeably explained and wine is decanted with a flourish. The ingredients used are the best the market can offer, from brochette of langoustines wrapped in bacon with dauphinois and fried green peppers, to partridge with a wild mushroom sauce. Puddings at La Yaya Amelia are great – try the fresh cheese bavarois with blackcurrants. Dilatory diners be warned, however; courses arrive at short intervals and simply accumulate.

Xocoa *p66* has a branch at C/Roger de Llúria 87 (93 487 2499).

Thai Gardens. *See p141.*

International

Al Diwan

C/Valencia 218, 08007 (93 454 07 12). Metro Passeig de Gràcia. **Meals served** 1-4pm, 8.30pm-midnight Mon-Fri; 8.30pm-midnight Sat. Closed Aug. **Average** €€. **Credit** AmEx, DC, MC, V.

Al Diwan is pure *Carry On Up the Lebanon* with a billowing tented ceiling, bright wool rugs on the walls, photos of bejewelled belly dancers, goatskins on the floor and dusky, mysterious lighting. The all-day special menu is fantastic value at just under €15, as is the excellent meze selection. Particularly outstanding dishes include the warak arich (stuffed vine leaves), tongue-twanging fatuch salad, spiced chicken wings and the kibe makile (wheat pancakes filled with onion, lamb and fried pine

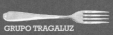

Just two blocks from the Sagrada Familia **La Yaya Amelia** p138 combines fresh-from-the-market cooking, with a fabulous wine list. Look out for its branch at C/Còrsega 537 (93 435 8048).

nuts). Finish off your meal with the aniseed-flavoured arak and, if it's a Friday or Saturday night, smile nervously at the doe-eyed dancing girls.

Le Relais de Venise

C/Pau Clarís 142, 08009 (93 467 21 62). Metro Passeig de Gràcia. **Meals served** 1.30-4pm, 8.30pm-12.30am Mon-Sat; 1.30-4pm, 8.30pm-midnight Sun. Closed Aug. **Average** €. **Credit** DC, MC, V.
Don't be surprised when you are ushered in, given a seat and asked how you want your steak done – that's all there is. A starter arrives in the shape of a green salad with walnuts, followed by a mountain of french fries and a slab of tender entrecôte. The special sauce is a closely guarded secret, but we can exclusively reveal the presence of tarragon. A woefully short wine list is also French (all four bottles), as is the list of puddings and cheese. The waitresses (nearly all of whom are also French) are dressed up in frilly black and white outfits, providing a rather peculiar contrast with the paper tablecloths, teak-effect pillars and battered mirrors.

Swan

C/Diputació 269, 08007 (93 488 09 77). Metro Passeig de Gràcia. **Meals served** 1-4pm, 8.30-11pm daily. **Average** €€€. **Credit** AmEx, DC, MC, V.
Swan is not your average Barcelona Chinese restaurant: no faux oriental decor, no lizardy spirits. The Chinese chef creates clean, careful flavours, while his Catalan wife treats the small, basement restaurant as her living room, and the clientele as old friends. Three times as expensive as other Chinese restaurants in Barcelona, Swan is certainly twice as good: steamed won ton are delicate and distinctive, noodles dishes are light and full of flavour. Spicy soup and spicy chicken are also good, though heat levels have been adjusted to the unadventurous Catalan palate. Quiet and intimate, it's not a place for the self-conscious.

Thai Gardens

C/Diputació 273, 08007 (93 487 98 98). Metro Passeig de Gràcia. **Meals served** 1.30-4pm, 8.30pm-midnight daily. **Average** €€. **Credit** AmEx, DC, MC, V.
A typically dramatic, but utterly convincing Thai restaurant, with fountains, palms, lilies, triangular floor cushions and waitresses in national dress. South-east Asian cuisine has yet to really catch on in Spain, and this is reflected in the unavailability of certain ingredients; key flavours missing are lemongrass and galangal, and there are some incongruous substitutions (celery features highly). The food is otherwise pretty good, although local tastes are reflected in the mildness of most curries. For something a little spicier, avoid the degustación, and pick the dishes with the heat warning signs from the à la carte.

Dry Martini. *See p148.*

Vegetarian

Arco Iris
*C/Roger de Flor 216, 08013 (93 458 22 83). Metro
Verdaguer.* **Meals served** 1.30-4pm Mon-Sat. Closed
Aug. **Average** €. **No credit cards**.
The noticeboard in this minty green corner joint is
feathered with flyers for rebirthing and crystal healing,
but if that's no great temptation, then just keep your eyes
on the menu. The lunch deal offers not two but three
imaginative savoury courses – such as pumpkin soup or
tofu chow mein, with many vegan dishes – and the
unusually wide choice of desserts includes own-made
pies and cheesecakes.

L'Atzavara
*C/Muntaner 109, 08036 (93 454 59 25). Metro Diagonal
or Hospital Clínic.* **Meals served** 1-4pm Mon-Sat.
Average €. **Credit** MC, V.
The set menu at this popular, friendly restaurant changes
daily and offers excellent value for money, with three
savoury courses of vegetarian classics, such as tofu
burgers and mushroom stroganoff, and a range of soups
and consommés. The restaurant marks 'light' dishes and
will remove any sauces or potatoes if you wish, although
no one should miss the wonderful own-made cakes.
Check the noticeboard to see if there's still a woman
offering macrobiotic cucumber massages.

Cafés & Bars

La Barcelonina de Vins i Esperits
*C/Valencia 304, 08009 (93 215 70 83). Metro Passeig de
Gràcia.* **Open** 6pm-2am Mon-Fri; 7.30pm-2am Fri, Sat.
Credit MC, V.
A wine and champagne lover's heaven. To the left is a wall
displaying the many varieties of wine available. To the
right is a bar, where you will be served post-haste. Straight
ahead, tables and, yet more important as the night wears
on, chairs. There is also a selection of meats and cheeses.

Bar Six
C/Muntaner 6, 08011 (93 453 00 75). Metro Universitat.
Open 8.30pm-3am Tue-Sat. Closed 2wks end Aug. **Credit**
AmEx, DC, MC, V.
Label fashion meets lava-lamp kitsch in this fashionable
bar paired with the equally popular restaurant next door,
Cosmopolita. A serious high-maintenance party crowd
charges up on good-time house and exotic cocktail shots
before migrating en masse to the night's main course.

The subject of
many a tourist
snap,
**Colmado
Quílez**
(Rambla
Catalunya 63)
is a gloriously
old-fashioned
looking
grocer's,
stacked to the
rafters with a
superb range
of food and
wine.

Come to Samoa and discover the freshest Mediterranean cuisine and our extraordinary specialities livened up by live piano music.
Enjoy the most exclusive terrace with a privileged view of "La Pedrera".

En Samoa podrá descubrir una fresca cocina mediterránea y unas tentadoras sugerencias amenizados por la noche con piano.
Disfrute de la más selecta terraza con privilegiadas vistas a "La Pedrera".

SAMOA

BAR ※ RESTAURANT ※ PIZZERIA
Pg. De Gràcia, 101   Tel. 93 218 47 82   08008 BARCELONA

La Bodegueta

Rambla de Catalunya 100, 08008 (93 215 48 94). Metro Diagonal/FGC Provença. **Open** 8am-2am Mon-Sat; 6.30pm-1am Sun. **No credit cards**.

Many of the elderly folk frequenting this little cellar bar have been coming here since their youth. A recent refurb has tidied it up a bit, while leaving the original rose petal tiles and old charm. It's especially crowded at lunchtime, with more suits and ties than overalls these days.

Café Torino

Passeig de Gràcia 59, 08007 (93 487 75 71). Metro Passeig de Gràcia. **Open** 8am-11pm Mon-Thur, Sun; 9am-1.30am Fri, Sat. **No credit cards**.

Jamón, jamón

From little acorns comes mighty ham. A lot of little acorns, mind you: between six and ten kilos per pig, per day. Many of the native Iberian pigs can exist on very little throughout the year, then, come autumn, they gorge themselves silly on unfeasible amounts of the things, and it is thanks to this that we have jamón de bellota, one of the tastiest cured hams in the world. Jamón de bellota comes from the cerdo ibérico, a small pig with a black coat and, often, black trotters. For this reason jamón ibérico is often known as pata negra (black foot), although the two are not strictly synonymous. Ham from a free-range ibérico pig fed on acorns is called de bellota; if the acorns are mixed with fodder, recebo, and if its diet is wholly cereals, pienso – all of which distinctions are reflected in the prices. The very best bellota, particularly that from Jabugo in Andalucia, can reach up to €160 a kilo.

Jamón ibérico accounts for only five per cent of Spain's vast output of ham, partly because of the difficulties of controlling free-range pigs, but also because the acorns come from a very specific source – a type of cork oak – and serious reforestation would be required before a marked increase in production could take place.

Slightly more affordable, and still one of the most delicious hams in the world, is jamón serrano, 'mountain ham': traditionally dried in the cold mountain air, but now normally kept in temperature-controlled cellars. Jamón serrano used to be used to describe all Spanish cured ham, but now refers solely to that which comes from white pigs, brought up in farmyards of Extremadura or Andalucia, and leaner and larger than their friends in the woodland. Like wine or cheese, jamones have their own denominaciones de origen; a good serrano DO to look out for is Teruel.

The original Café Torino, a wonderful Modernista flight of fancy, only exists in the fading photographs on the walls; whether they are there to boast of its glorious past or as a sackcloth for mindless '60s destruction is unclear. This place is a useful refuelling stop on visits to more fortunate architectural gems, with decent coffee and good bocadillos.

Casa Alfonso

C/Roger de Llúria 6, 08010 (93 301 97 83). Metro Urquinaona. **Open** 8am-1am Mon-Fri; noon-1am Sat. Closed 2wks Aug. **Credit** AmEx, DC, MC, V.
In the same family since it opened back in 1935, Casa Alfonso has a refined, old-fashioned air; monochrome murals of early 20th-century Barcelona decorate the walls, hams hang from the high ceiling, and glass-fronted cupboards display rows of bottles of oil and wine. Locals pop in for fine tapas and the selection of embotits and other charcuterie. There are more tables in the room at the back amid the exhibition of slightly questionable art.

Pastisseria Mauri (Rambla Catalunya 102) opened in 1885 and is still selling delicate cakes and sandwiches to eat in or take away.

Out of town

Catalonia's natural charms – rolling hills, snow-tipped mountains, picturesque villages and magnificent coastline – have made it a magnet both for tourists and wealthy second-homers. Apart from along certain stretches of the coastline, however, the effect on rural life has been almost imperceptible; except, that is, for the phenomenal amount of superb restaurants dotted around the countryside.

The best known, of course, is the legendary **El Bulli** (*see p49*), up near Roses on the Costa Brava. Following hard on its heels is the superb **El Racó de Can Fabes** (C/Sant Joan 6, Sant Celoni, 93 867 28 51/www.racocanfabes.com), a luxurious but refreshingly unpretentious place at the foot of the Montseny mountains, and widely seen as one of Spain's top restaurants.

Within easy reach of Barcelona are several lesser-known gems; **L'Esguard** (Passatge de les Alzines 16, Sant Andreu de Llavaneres; 93 792 77 67) is half an hour's drive from the city, just off the C32. In a lovely old farmhouse, Argentinian chef Miguel Sánchez indulges his passion for food by creating daring and spectacular dishes from Catalan standards when he's not at his day job as head of neurology at a nearby hospital. A little further along, perched unpromisingly on the side of a main road near Arenys de Mar, is **Hispània** (Crta Reial 54, 93 791 04

Eixample

Cervecería Catalana

C/Mallorca 236, 08008 (93 216 0368). Metro Passeig de Gràcia. **Open** 7.30pm-1.30am Mon-Fri; 9pm-1.30am Sat, Sun. **Credit** AmEx, DC, MC, V.

A professional, slightly upmarket treatment of the traditional tapas bar – perfect for those looking for the tapas experience but who aren't sure they're ready for sawdust on the floor. Cervecería Catalana offers a fantastic selection of tapas at mid-range prices.

Domèstic

C/Diputació 215, 08011 (93 453 16 61). Metro Universitat. **Open** 7pm-2.30am Tue-Thur; 7pm-3am Fri-Sun. **Credit** AmEx, DC, MC, V.

Yet another of the rash of bar-club-restaurants to hit the city, here with the emphasis on the drinking side of things, Domèstic has chilled music, bold colours and battered leather chairs and sofas, which give it an appealingly laid-back and lived-in atmosphere. Token food is served in the dining room at the front between 9pm and midnight.

57), famed, among other things, for its magnificent bodega (winery) and what is allegedly the best pa amb tomàquet in Catalonia.

The next town along the coast (and one of the more unspoilt fishing towns of the Costa Brava) is Sant Pol, home to celebrated chef Carme Ruscalleda and her restaurant **Sant Pau** (Nou 10, 93 760 06 62). Here, as in Hispània, the speciality is cuina de mercat (market cuisine), which basically means the very finest produce that local farms and the Mediterranean have to offer. Further proof that the greatest chefs are not all men lies a mere 20km away at **Les Petxines** (Hotel Excelsior, Passeig Mossèn J

Verdaguer 16, 97 236 41 37), where Paula Casanovas continues to dazzle.

The other rich culinary seam is the area around Vic. In the town itself expect such delights as cod tripe in a liquorice soup or pigeon and banana risotto at elegant **Jordi Parramon** (C/Cardona 7, 93 886 38 15), while, just outside, Can Jubany (Ctra Sant Hilari, Calldetenes, *93 889 10 23*) is truly outstanding and equally inventive. Others to look out for within a short drive of Vic include **Fonda Sala** (Plaça Mayor 4, Olost, 93 888 01 06), and the excellent **Lluçanès** (Major 1, Prats de Lluçanès; 93 850 80 50/ www.restaurantllucanes.com) – both offer superb game dishes and encyclopaedic wine lists.

Eixample

Dry Martini ★

C/Aribau 162-6, 08036 (93 217 50 72). FCG Provença.
Open 6.30pm-2.30am Mon-Thur, Sun; 6.30pm-3am Fri,
Sat. **Credit** AmEx, DC, MC, V.

This wonderful bar has all the trappings of a trad cocktail
bar: bow-tied staff, leather banquettes, the odd drinking
antique and wooden cabinets displaying a century's worth
of bottles. Yet despite the formality there's no stuffiness; the
music is gently groovy and the barmen welcome all comers.

La Fira

C/Provença 171, 08036 (no phone). Metro Hospital Clínic.
Open 10pm-3am Mon-Thur; 10.30pm-4.30am Fri, Sat.
No credit cards.

The **Comme
Bio** restaurant
chain has a
branch at
Gran Via de
les Corts
Catalanes
603 (93 301
0376).

La Fira

Enter La Fira through the corridor lined with crazy mirrors to a warehouse-sized space filled with an extraordinarily haphazard collection of old funfair detritus: merry-go-round horses, one-armed bandits, crazy mirrors and more. Out of their environment of childhood innocence, these can seem a little macabre; grotesquely smiling clowns' faces leer at the beefcake barmen, the new masters of the big top, as they dish out drinks to a raucous studenty crowd revelling to the sounds of tacky pop.

Les Gens Que J'Aime

C/Valencia 286, 08007 (93 215 68 79). Metro Passeig de Gràcia. **Open** 7pm-3am Mon-Sat; 7pm-2.30am Sun. **No credit cards.**

Les Gens Que J'Aime. *See p149.*

Ageing red velvet sofas and antique lamps casting a dim
light make the patrons look mysterious and bohemian –
an optical illusion only, for the location means the clientele
are largely middle-aged and middle-class locals. Still, it's
a great place for a quiet, unhurried drink and, in keeping
with the bohemian theme, a tarot card reader holds court.

La Gran Bodega
*C/Valencia 193, 08011 (93 453 10 53). Metro Passeig
de Gràcia or Universitat.* **Open** 11am-1am Tue-Sun.
Credit MC, V.

An old-fashioned bar with tall ceilings, wine barrels and all manner of knick-knacks: porrones, terracotta plates decorated with pearls of drinking wisdom, photos of Barça players past and present, wooden clogs and cartwheels. The draught Kronenbourg and good tapas go down well with a studenty crowd, who also appear to enjoy the loud technopop.

Laie Libreria Café

C/Pau Claris 85, 08010 (93 302 73 10). Metro Urquinaona. **Open** *Café* 9am-1am Mon-Fri; 10am-1am Sat. *Bookshop* 10.30am-9pm Mon-Sat. **Credit** AmEx, DC, MC, V.

The layout at the front of Laie Libreria Café is a little cramped, but the covered patio at the back is the perfect spot to unwind: airy, spacious and decorated with photographs of last century's literary giants. There is a buffet breakfast of pastries, eggs, fruit and bocadillos, a light lunch menu and more substantial fare at night. If nothing takes your fancy in the bookshop downstairs, there's a great selection of magazines and papers to read.

La Pedrera de Nit

C/Provença 261-5, 08008 (93 484 59 95). Metro Diagonal. **Open** 9pm-midnight Fri, Sat. Closed Oct-June. *Admission* (incl 1 drink) €9. **Credit** MC, V.

In summer, the swerving, rolling roof terrace of Gaudí's visionary La Pedrera is open on Friday and Saturday evenings for drinks, live music and fine views of the city, but it's essential to book.

The Pop Bar

C/Aribau 103, 08036 (93 451 29 58). Metro Hospital Clínic/FCG Provença. **Open** 6pm-3.30am Wed-Sun. **Credit** AmEx, DC, MC, V.

The Pop Bar gets full marks for its '70s retro decor: red leather pouffes and geometric patterns in the browns and oranges last seen in *Austin Powers*. Musically, it could use some direction, playing neither period glam-rock classics, nor up-to-the-minute beats, but instead stuck in a land of europop. The young but mildly conservative-looking bunch who come here seem happy, however.

Santécafé

C/Comte d'Urgell 171, 08036 (93 323 78 32). Metro Hospital Clínic. **Open** 8am-3am Mon-Fri; 5pm-3am Sat, Sun. **No credit cards.**

Cool but sociable locals hang out until late in this stylish night café with a clued-up music policy. With low lighting, immaculate grooves from what used to be called acid jazz to funky hip hop to deep house, and plenty of tables, Santé is the kind of place you can arrange to meet before going on somewhere else – and end up staying.

Branches of **Tragaluz** *p136* (where Javier Mariscal designed the menus) can be found at **El Japonés** Passatge de la Concepció 2 (93 487 2592); **Negro** Avda Diagonal 640 (*93 405 9444*); **El Principal** C/Provença 286 (93 272 0845).

The Pop Bar

Seltz

C/Rosselló 154, 08036 (93 453 38 42). Metro Hospital Clínic. **Open** 9pm-3am Wed-Sat. **Credit** AmEx, MC, V.
The latest to jump on the club-bar-restaurant gravy train, Seltz is now principally a funky place for a drink, with a colourful award-winning interior. A resident DJ spins lounge and chillout early on and deep house once the tables are cleared and the diners dancing.

Stinger

C/Còrsega 338, 08037 (93 217 71 87). Metro Diagonal. **Open** 6.30pm-3am Mon-Thur; 6.30pm-3.30am Fri, Sat. **Credit** MC, V.
For a place so firmly entrenched in the Barcelona scene, Stinger doesn't take itself too seriously. Sure, the glossy black bar, velvet seating and moody yellow lighting are cocktail-bar cliché, but the unwritten rule that only Brazilian bossa should be played is flouted routinely, and not always fortuitously. Prepare to rock.

Valor Chocolatería

Rambla Catalunya 46, 08007 (93 487 62 46). Metro Passeig de Gràcia. **Open** 8.30am-12.30pm, 4.30-11pm Mon-Fri; 9am-1am Sat, Sun. **No credit cards**.
From chocolate fondues with a plate of fruit for dunking to the standard steaming mugful, chocolate in all its guises is taken very seriously here. Cabinets full of own-made sweets lure in passers-by.

Seltz

Gràcia

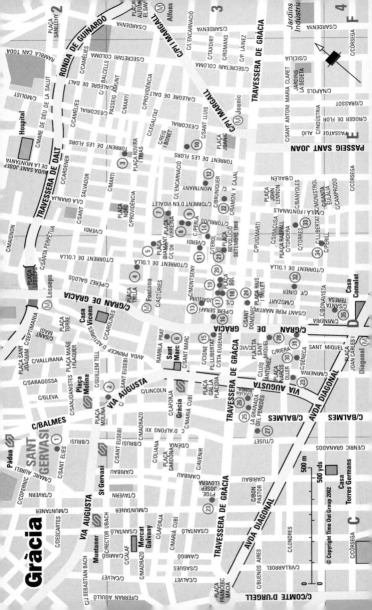

Restaurants

Bilbao de Gràcia ★

C/Perill 33, 08012 (93 458 96 24). Metro Diagonal or Verdaguer. **Meals served** 1-4pm, 9-11pm daily. Closed Aug. **Average** €€€. **No credit cards.**

A great place to eat, especially in good company. The restaurant is in a traditional Castilian mesón style, although the menu is mainstream Catalan and Spanish with a twist. Vegetarian starters are excellent, as is the jumbo prawn salad. Main courses include fresh seafood – the Palamòs gambas (prawns) are particularly recommended – and rich, succulent meats such as roast leg of lamb or, unusually, steak from a fighting bull. Desserts are a little more conventional. Bilbao is also a smoker's haven, with pipes, cigars, roll-ups and plain old cigarettes mellowing the air.

Botafumeiro

C/Gran de Gràcia 81, 08012 (93 218 42 30/ www.botafumeiro.es). Metro Fontana. **Meals served** 1pm-1am daily. Closed 3wks Aug. **Average** €€€€. **Credit** AmEx, MC, V.

Reports both ecstatic and excoriating continue to fly in on this legendary seafood restaurant, but we found the service excellent and the shellfish divine. The efficiency of the operation (all 300 seats are almost permanently occupied) is staggering, but is also Botafumeiro's least likeable aspect. Squadrons of waiters in white jackets with gold nautical trim to match the gilt-edged decor; menus in a host of languages; every last cubic metre of space put to good use – all these things add up to a rather impersonal experience. Still, the seafood is the thing; the juicy salpicón de bogavante y mariscos (lobster and shellfish salad) is superbly fresh and consummately dressed, and the fish dishes are worth trying too. Sea bass is baked, smothered in onions, mushrooms, garlic and flat-leaf parsley. Sole is served in a delicious buttery cava sauce with langoustines. It's not cheap (and there's a huge mark-up on wines), but it's good.

La Buena Tierra

C/Encarnació 56, 08024 (93 219 82 13). Metro Joanic. **Meals served** 1-4pm, 8pm-midnight Mon-Sat. Closed 2wks July-Aug. **Average** €. **Credit** MC, V.

An uncomplicated, unpretentious restaurant serving reasonable, though by no means outstanding, food in a small (slightly) converted ground-floor flat. The restaurant's charming garden is perfect on summer evenings. The menu is typical Catalan farmhouse: cannelloni, torrades (*see p59* **Slices of life**) with cheese

Gràcia

Basque
Amaya (see p25); **Euskal Extea** (see p118) and **Laurak** (see p161).

Catalan
Cafè de l'Acadèmia (see p27); **Can Travi Nou** (see p205); **Casa Calvet** (see p129); **Octubre** (see p161); **La Parra** (see p198) and **Windsor** (see p137).

Italian
La Bella Napoli (see p200); **Figaro** (see p164), and **Specchio Magico** (see p169).

Japanese
Machiroku (see p41); **Shunka** (see p43); **SoNaMu** (see p168) and **Tokyo** (see p45).

Latin American
Cantina Machito (see p163); **El Celler de Macondo** (see p111); **Habana Vieja** (see p111); **El Paraguayo** (see p43) and **Peimong** (see p43).

Middle Eastern
Al Diwan (see p139); **Habibi** (see p165) and **Mesopotamia** (see p165).

Southeast Asian
Govinda (see p45); **Lahore** (see p165) and **Thai Gardens** (see p141).

or sausage, meat cooked on wood coals and a reasonably good list of vegetarian options. A good-value menú del día caters for both vegetarians and meat-eaters. Textured soya comes with a rich cheese sauce; spinach cannelloni is a good bet, as is the grilled rabbit.

La Cova d'en Vidalet
C/Torrent d'en Vidalet 22, 08012 (93 213 55 30). Metro Fontana or Joanic. **Meals served** 1.30-3.30pm Mon; 1.30-3.30pm, 9-11pm Tue-Thur; 9pm-midnight Fri, Sat. Closed 3wks Sept. **Average** €€. **Credit** MC, V.
This street is crammed with tiny eateries but Cova d'en Vidalet is one of the best. Small, quiet and simple, its plain walls are softened by a couple of high mirrors and buttery yellow lighting. Service is exceptionally friendly here. The lunch menu is incredibly good value at €6.60

Gràcia

and includes leafy salads, salmon steaks and a gourmet version of a cheeseburger and french fries that's cheap enough to have Ronald McDonald quaking in his boots. The imaginative à la carte selection is more upmarket, with highlights such as tagliatelle with a foie gras mousse, partridge salad, monkfish ragoût with porcini mushrooms, or hake en papillote.

Envalira

Plaça del Sol 13, 08012 (93 218 58 13). Metro Fontana.
Meals served 1.30-4pm, 9pm-midnight Tue-Sat; 1.30-5pm
Sun. Closed Aug. **Average** €€. **Credit** AmEx, MC, V.
Get to Envalira as it opens for a squidgy leather banquette near the bar at the front, otherwise you'll be relegated to the school room at the back where you could find yourself sharing a table with four strangers. In decor terms, Envalira is no looker with its Artex-coated walls, stone cladding painted brown and energy-saving lightbulbs, but there is a really decent selection of regional favourites from Catalonia, Galicia, the Basque Country and other parts of Spain. These include several types of fish cooked in several different ways; thick, tender steaks; game dishes of all kinds and stack-'em-high salads. This is a good place, too, to try out traditional Spanish desserts, such as crema catalana, tarta de Santiago and flan. Like everything else here they are own-made, delicious and keenly priced.

Gràcia

El Glop. *See p160*

El Glop

C/Montmany 46, 08012 (93 213 70 58). Metro Joanic.
Meals served 1-4pm, 8pm-1am Tue-Sun. **Average** €€.
Credit MC, V.
This long-running Gracià institution is housed in a rambling building with low beams upstairs and a kind of indoor patio with a retractable roof downstairs. The specialities are traditional char-grilled meat (try the succulent filete de ternera) washed down with fearsome Priorat reds drunk from a glass porró (jug), and snails baked a la llauna. The suquet de rape (monkfish stew) arrives sizzling in a terracotta dish and is enough for two.

Jean Luc Figueras ★

C/Santa Teresa 10, 08012 (93 415 28 77). Metro Diagonal. **Meals served** 1.30-3.30pm, 8.30-11.30pm Mon-Fri; 8.30-11.30pm Sat. Closed 2wks Aug. **Average** €€€€.
Credit AmEx, DC, MC, V.
Jean Luc Figueras's quiet, luxurious restaurant occupies the former studio of haute-couturier Balenciaga. Figueras provides his own brand of Catalan-French couture and his perfectly executed classics are rendered unforgettable

through wonderful sauces and innovative combinations, such as roast guinea fowl with cardamom. The long menú degustación is perfectly balanced. Highlights include a salad of partridge, black truffle, and foie gras with Armagnac prunes, Laguiole fondue with bonito brochettes, or red mullet escabeche marinated with orange. Desserts, such as the parfait of peanuts and caramelised banana with milk chocolate sorbet, are sumptuous. A superb cheese board, wine list and range of cigars are available, as well as a smoking lounge and two private dining rooms.

Laurak ★
C/Granada del Penedès 14-16, 08006 (93 218 71 65).
FCG Gràcia. **Meals served** 1-4pm, 9-11.30pm Mon-Sat.
Average €€€. Credit AmEx, DC, MC, V.
A sleek, ocean-liner cocktail bar opens out to a spacious dining room given warmth by red table linen, soft lighting and attentive service. Laurak's renowned menu includes Basque specialities such as black pudding from Besain and Idiazábal cheese. Imaginatively crafted combinations such as duck foie gras with toffee-glazed slices of banana, or red mullet with a sesame crust and black olive vinaigrette, are also on offer. Puddings are supremely luxurious; try the pistachio biscuit with praline mousse and chocolate crocante. The menú degustación is really excellent value – try it with a bottle of white Txakoli.

Octubre ★
C/Julián Romea 18, 08006 (93 218 25 18). FCG Gràcia.
Meals served 1.30-3.30pm, 9-11pm Mon-Fri; 9-11pm Sat.
Closed Aug. **Average €. Credit** MC, V.
This tiny temple to Catalan cuisine is always full, and with good reason. The improbably low-priced dishes change according to what's in season. Starters include sizzling patates eivissenques (Ibizan potatoes) with clams, little green peppers and sobrassada (Mallorcan spicy sausage). Tortilla with haricot beans and amanida carnestoltes (carnival salad) with escarola lettuce, botifarra and romesco sauce are also recommended. To follow, estofat d'ànec al vi negre (duck stew with red wine) comes with cabbage and a tasty mushroom sauce. Tender corvall (sea bass) is served on a bed of young garlic and onions. On St Joseph's day (19 March), we were given a slice of local speciality pastis de Sant Josep, an exquisite crema catalana turned cheesecake, served with strawberries. Octubre is something of a one-man show, so expect quite a long wait for the food to arrive, but it is worth every minute.

Ot ★
C/Torres 25, 08012 (93 284 77 52). Metro Diagonal or
Verdaguer. **Meals served** 2-3.30pm, 9-10.30pm Mon-Fri;
9-10.30pm Sat. Closed 3wks Aug. **Average €€€€.**
Credit AmEx, MC, V.

La Buena Tierra *p157* offers typical Catalan farmhouse cooking, as does its branch at **La Llar de Foc** C/Ramón y Cajal 13 (*93 284 10 25*).

Gràcia

When Ot first opened, its six tables were among the most sought-after in town. Then came the backlash. The funky paintwork, colourful mobiles and gamelan soundtrack were considered gimmicky, but now Ot is creeping back into fashion. Nowhere else in Barcelona can you get food this good in such a fresh, relaxed atmosphere. There is no menu; waiters are happy to make recommendations. Among Ot's best dishes are prawn tempura with curry foam, tuna tataki wrapped in a gossamer-thin sheet of pineapple, or ravioli of smoked aubergine served with

Take it away

The Spanish more or less invented fast food. You point to what you want, the waiter scrapes, spoons or slices it on to your plate and that's it. Have a nice day. It seems incredible that Old McDonald and his farm should have got their beefy grasp on the nation's diet, but they have. Fortunately, when you want something to eat on the move, there are plenty of other things to choose from. Two chains of sandwich and salad outlets, Pans & Company and Bocatta, both serving reasonably nutritious food and with menus available in English, can be found all over the city. For a more personal and interesting sandwich, **Bar Kasparo** (see p86) in a pretty square near the top of the Ramblas is good, as is nearby **Buenas Migas** (see p52), which serves delicious focaccia, pasta salads and lasagne to eat in or take away ('para llevar'). For more traditional sandwiches and tapas, nearby **Bar Castell** (Plaça Bonsuccés 1, 93 302 10 54) or the **Bar del Pi** (see p51) over in the Barri Gòtic are both good. All four cafés also

have pleasant outdoor tables. At the other end of the old city, **Sandwich & Friends** (Passeig del Born 27, 93 310 07 86) has exciting sandwiches to eat in or take away, while **La Pizza del Born** at No.22 (93 310 62 46) does slices of pizza.

Finally, the kebab has infiltrated Barcelona, particularly around Plaça Reial and C/Verdi in Gràcia – just follow your nose. All the places serving them also serve falafel, and are open from 8am to 1am. **Buen Bocado** (C/Escudellers 31, 93 317 27 91) has a good reputation for kebabs and falafel, but is tiny and always packed. As an alternative, **Maos Falafel** (C/Ferran 13, 93 412 12 61) just does falafel, to which you add your own garnishes. For a slightly more upmarket kebab served with tsatsiki, houmous or taramasalata, as well as sit-down Greek food, **Dionisos** has four outlets in the city, including one in the Born (Avda Marqués de Argentera 27, 93 268 24 72) and another in Gràcia (C/Torrent de l'Olla 144). There are ways to beat the burger.

pancetta in a turrón 'soup'. Spectacular puddings include thyme ice-cream with a balsamic vinegar reduction. Coffee comes with shotglasses of tangy passion fruit mousse.

El Racó d'en Freixa

C/Sant Elies, 22, 08006 (93 209 75 59). FGC Plaça Molina. **Open** 1-3.30pm, 9-11.30pm Tue-Sat; 1-3.30pm Mon. Closed Aug. **Average** €€€€. **Credit** AmEx, DC, MC, V.

A young, highly acclaimed chef of talent and creativity, Ramon Freixa is slightly let down by details. Service is somewhat panicked and discriminatory; bread doesn't always taste fresh and decor is drab. A pity, for there are some interesting things coming out of the kitchen, from tiny roquefort fairy cakes and miniature cones holding chorizo mousse, to a chocolate dessert featuring chocolate mousse, cocoa bean brittle, café con leche ice-cream and a spicy tomato confit. Other delights include a cappuccino de pularda; a ravioli of poularde in its own soup with a cloud of creamy foam, and the mezcla de verduras; a stack of lightly steamed vegetables sprinkled with pansy petals and served with romesco ice-cream. One to watch out for.

Roig Robí

C/Sèneca 20, 08006 (93 218 92 22). Metro Diagonal. **Meals served** 1.30-4pm, 9-11.30pm Mon-Fri; 9-11.30pm Sat. Closed 2wks Aug. **Average** €€€€. **Credit** AmEx, DC, MC, V.

Calm, airy dining rooms, with sea grass matting, lead to a garden terrace at the back. It's all very Zen, except on quiet nights when patrolling waiters can be unsettling – like dining out under police escort. The menu is short but wide in scope, with fish, meat, game and rice. The speciality are the gambas de Palamòs con crujiente de puerros (Palamòs prawns with crispy shredded leek). Duck breast with creamed pistachio sauce is also excellent. Vieiras (scallops) and mango salad make a tangy, light starter, but leave enough room for desserts: the yoghurt cream with apple ice-cream and Calvados jelly is not to be missed.

International

Cantina Machito

C/Torrijos 47, 08012 (93 217 34 14). Metro Fontana or Joanic. **Meals served** 1-4.30pm, 7pm-1.30am daily. **Average** €. **Credit** MC, V.

The most authentic Mexican restaurant in the city, family-run Cantina Machito serves great classics such as mole poblano (shredded turkey breast smothered in a chilli mole sauce) and tender lamb al pastor, accompanied by beans, salsas and salads. For dessert, the lime and tequila mousse is to die for. The family also holds big celebrations on Mexican national holidays, when you can try pan de muertos ('bread of the dead') and rare tequilas.

Gràcia

Bodega Manolo. *See p169.*

Figaro

C/Ros de Olano 4 bis, 08012 (93 237 43 53). Metro Fontana. **Meals served** 1.30-4pm, 8.30pm-1am Mon, Wed-Fri; 1.30-4pm Tue; 8.30pm-1am Sat, Sun. **Average** €. **Credit** MC, V.

This popular 'spaghetteria' serves simple, elegant Italian meals in a delightfully intimate setting. The lunchtime menú del dia (€8.50) offers authentic pastas and salads and refreshingly light main courses such as paper-thin slices of rare roast beef. At night the à la carte menu opens with imaginative salads combining such delicious ingredients as rocket and provolone, or pear and parmesan. Popular spaghetti sauces at Figaro include spicy puttanesca (with tomatoes, olives, capers and chilli) and ragu. The carpaccios, either veal or salmon, are strong favourites with the steady stream of groovy locals. Panna cotta or superb platters of Italian cheeses provide the perfect finale.

La Gavina

C/Ros de Olano 17, 08012 (93 415 74 50). Metro Fontana. **Meals served** 8pm-2am Tue; 2pm-2am Wed-Sun. **Average** €. **No credit cards**.

Gina and Marina dish out fantastic own-made ice-cream until 2am at **Il Gelato Artigianale Italiano** (Plaça Revolució de Setembre 1868, 2); the chocolate and hazelnut is to die for.

Hearty pizzas and a relaxed atmosphere make La Gavina the perfect place for a speedy, substantial pizza fix. Pizzas at this popular joint come with fresh toppings and a good crisp base. Tables are tiny and tightly packed and the restaurant is also notable for its unusual decor. Dozens of angels decorate the ceilings and walls, along with an unusual mix of matador outfits, guns and a giant hand. Served on wooden platters, the pizzas range from plainish tomato and mozzarella, through to pulpo (octopus) or Hawaiian (ham, pineapple, prawns and caviar). There are several good traditional choices in between and a wide range of vegetarian options.

Habibi

C/Gran de Gràcia 7, 08012 (93 217 95 45). Metro Diagonal. **Meals served** 1pm-1am Mon-Fri; 2-4pm, 8pm-2am Sat. **Average** €. **Credit** AmEx, DC, MC, V.

Habibi ('my darling' in Arabic) is a refuge of calm from the noisy Gràcia traffic, with winding plants and trickling waterfalls. Welcoming owner Hassan is one of the few people in Barcelona to use organic meats and vegetables. As well as classic shawarmas and falafels, there are more elaborate dishes such as kube halabi (spiced lamb in a sealed semolina pancake with fruits and nuts) or matabal aubergine dip. The wide and inventive range of vegetarian dishes includes stuffed vine leaves, couscous salads and urugi burgers with houmous.

Lahore

C/Torrent de l'Olla 159, 08012 (93 218 95 11). Metro Fontana. **Meals served** midday-4pm, 8pm-midnight Tue-Sun. **Average** €. **Credit** V.

If you get past the Kodak birianis and samosas festooned all over the windows, you've still got to face the plastic nosegays shining brightly in the neon glow of economy lightbulbs and daytime TV. It's all worth it, however, as the food is far superior to many Pakistani joints downtown and the prices are very reasonable: only €7.5 for the all-in lunch menu, which includes coffee. Crunchy golden chapatis, creamy kormas, excellent onion bhajis and a killer prawn mughlai stand out among a huge range of classics from the capital of the Punjab.

Mesopotamia

C/Verdi 65, 08012 (93 237 15 63). Metro Fontana. **Meals served** 8.30pm-midnight Mon-Sat. **Average** €. **Credit** MC, V.

The terracotta and adobe decor gives a Temple of Doom effect to Barcelona's only Iraqi restaurant. You almost expect Indiana Jones to come bursting out from behind the wonderful ziggurat friezes. Owner Pius has done an equally excellent job with the menu, which is based on Arab 'staff of life' foods, such as yoghurt and rice. Best

Gràcia

value is the enormous taster menu, which includes great Lebanese wines, a variety of dips for your riqaq bread, such as tamr wa laban (toffee-sweet date sauce with onion, cumin and walnuts), aromatic roast meats, sticky baklava and Arabic teas.

La Nueva Rosa del Desierto

Plaça Narcís Oller, 08006 (93 237 45 90). Metro Diagonal. **Meals served** 1-3.30pm, 9-11.30pm Mon-Sat; 1-3.30pm Sun. **Average** €€. **Credit** AmEx, DC, MC, V.
Desert Rose refers not to a flower but to an odd formation of encrusted desert sand resembling petals (there's an example inside). The restaurant offers exclusively Moroccan cuisine, recalling a time well before mass immigration when North Africa was far away, exotic, and thus justifiably pricey. Couscous, accompanied by a light broth with chickpeas, is the speciality, and here it is particularly well done. Part of the menu is presented

At **La Bellota** (C/Escorial 30) you'll find some of the very finest hams in the country; every denominación de origen region in Spain is represented.

SoNaMu. *See p168.*

Taking the strain

Although tea has little chance of making a dent in Barcelona's firmly entrenched coffee culture, something is definitely brewing. The teterías (tea houses) sprouting up around the city provide a much-needed alternative to the mass-produced blends offered at your average café. In Barcelona, the sawdusty Hornimans brand is ubiquitous, and generally served black or with lemon; if you want a milky cuppa, then ask first for a tea, and request the milk separately afterwards, otherwise you're likely to end up with a bemused waiter and a teabag floating in a glass of longlife UHT. Herbal teas are not té but infusiones, and those most available are manzanilla (camomile), poleomenta (mint) and tila (lime or linden blossom.)

For something fancier, try one of the following: with branches in Gràcia and the Barri Gòtic, **Teashaker** (C/Santa Creu 5, 93 415 00 59, or C/Ferran 39) serves sushi snacks and gourmet iced teas in funky, minimalist surroundings. House specialities are the black and green teas with unusual toppings such as fresh fruit, wheatgerm or frogspawny tapioca pearls. Nearby, just off the Plaça del Sol, **Jazmin** (C/Maspons 11, 93 218 71 84) is an intimate Tunisian restaurant and tearoom with exotic oriental decor, and teas such as apple, orange blossom and sage and mint, as well as relaxing tisanes.

In the Raval, try **Ayub** (C/Hospital 95, 93 442 54 29) a tiny Arabic pastry shop where you can wash down the house speciality of gooey baklava with fresh mint tea.

The Barri Gòtic has the highest concentration of tea places, and **Salterio** (C/Sant Domènec del Call 4, 93 302 50 28, is a real find: a tiny, mysterious, Arabian-style tea bar that's buzzing with neighbourhood bohemians. Try Salterio's speciality of vegetarian 'sardo' pitta snacks, along with teas such as wild strawberry, maté, star anise or the complex 16-leaf blend, té mu.

La Clandestina (C/Baixada de Viladecols, 2 bis, no phone, open 9am-10pm Mon-Thur, 9am-12pm Fri, Sat) is a mellow, New Age hangout with chunky own-made cakes, and a huge range of teas including massala xai, lotus flower, or cherry and redcurrant. Its small shop stocks many blends, plus a selection of tea-related paraphernalia, and on Friday and Saturday nights there is often a trapeze act along with live music.

Attracting a slightly alternative clientele, the two-tiered, rainbow-coloured **La Tete** (C/Comtessa de Sobradiel 4, 93 268 45 33) stocks some tannin-free teas, along with everything from smoky Lapsang Souchong to blends with names like English Rose, Moonlight and Hawaiian Cocktail.

Gràcia

Mond Bar. *See p171.*

as macrobiotic, and indeed the vegetable dishes are more reliable than the somewhat overcooked lamb – and generally better priced. Round off your meal with a typical honey-based dessert and fresh mint tea.

SoNaMu

Passatge Josep Llovera 11, 08021 (93 209 65 83). FCG Muntaner. **Meals served** 1.30-3.30pm, 8.30-11.30pm Mon-Sat. **Average** €. **Credit** DC, MC, V.

SoNaMu offers Korean and Japanese specialities of consistently good quality. The dolsot is a searingly hot stone bowl filled with rice, meat and vegetables. There are also different kinds of sushi and a selection of Korean-style barbecued meat. If you want a quick, healthy lunch, try one of the bento boxes: each contains four or five treats, such as steamed gyoza dumplings, a stack of vegetable and prawn tempura, sushi, sashimi, wasabi, and seaweed and noodle salad.

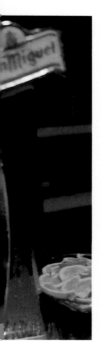

Specchio Magico

C/Luis Antúnez 3, 08006 (93 415 33 71). Metro Diagonal or Fontana. **Meals served** 2-4pm, 9-11pm Mon-Sat; 2-4pm Sun. **Average** €€€. **Credit** AmEx, DC, MC, V.

Wall-to-wall wood panelling covered in postcards and framed letters may make Specchio Magico look a little like the rumpus room at a Moose Lodge, but the warm and friendly service more than make up for such shortcomings. No pizzas are served here, but the four Italian chef/owners offer pasta dishes of the highest quality, from rigatoni alla puttanesca to sedanini with truffles and foie gras. Portions are gigantic. There's also a solid selection of Italian and Spanish wines, plus excellent meat dishes and traditional desserts, such as own-made panna cotta and tiramisù.

Vegetarian

L'Illa de Gràcia

C/Sant Doménech 19, 08012 (93 238 02 29). Metro Diagonal. **Meals served** 1-4pm, 9pm-midnight Tue-Fri; 2-4pm, 9pm-midnight Sat, Sun. Closed late Aug. **Average** €. **Credit** DC, MC, V.

The minimalist decor, dark wooden slab tables and exposed brick walls make L'Illa de Gràcia one of the few vegetarian restaurants in Barcelona to make any concession to style or ambience. The extensive menu features no fewer than 14 different salads. The restaurant also offers dishes such as pan-fried tofu with alfalfa and wild rice, filled crêpes, own-made cakes and fruit puddings. All are excellent value for money.

Cafés & Bars

La Baignoire

C/Verdi 4, 08012 (615 45 80 22). Metro Fontana. **Open** 7pm-3am Mon, Wed-Sun. **No credit cards.**

As white and gleaming as a bathtub and not much bigger, La Baignoire still manages to be comfortable, with slide projections and lounge music complementing the cool mellow vibe. Simple tapas and smiles from the staff are always available.

Bodega Manolo

C/Torrent de les Flors 101, 08024 (93 284 43 77). Metro Joanic. **Open** 12.30-4.30pm, 8pm-12.30am Tue-Sat; 12.30am-4.30pm Sun. Closed Aug. **No credit cards.**

Don't be alarmed. The dusty paint curlicues hanging from the ceiling could only be classified as unhygienic if one of them fell into your foie gras with port and apple. The atmosphere, classifiable as grim if you're peeking in from the street, is friendly and comfortable inside, and those old barrels lining the walls really are filled with wine. Full evening meals are served from Thursday to Saturday.

Café del Sol

Plaça del Sol 16, 08012 (93 415 56 63). Metro Fontana. **Open** 1pm-2.30am Mon-Thur, Sun; 1pm-3am Fri, Sat. **No credit cards.**

Nursing a long drink on the terrace as the cadent sun casts shadows across Gràcia's liveliest square is heavenly. Being stuffed inside on a winter's night is an acquired taste. The three-deep bar is noisy, boisterous, but still kind of fun.

Casa Quimet

Rambla de Prat 9, 08012 (93 217 53 27). Metro Fontana. **Open** 6.30pm-2am Tue-Sun. Closed Feb, Aug. **No credit cards.**

Known locally as the 'guitar bar', Casa Quimet has more than 200 guitars lining the walls. You're welcome to grab one and join in the jamming session. From the faded black and white photos to the gloomy greenness of this down-and-out bar, there is not a single polished element here.

Flash Flash

C/Granada del Penedès 25, 08006 (93 237 09 90). FGC Gràcia. **Open** 1pm-1am daily. **Credit** AmEx, DC, MC, V.

Flash back to the '60s with white leatherette banquettes, walls lined with life-size photos of a Twiggyesque model and a kitschfest on the stereo. Opened in 1970, this bar was a design sensation in its day and the owners never saw the need to change with the times. Decades passed and – what do you know! – it's suddenly hip again. They call it a tortilleria, and they mean it, with more than 50 variations on the theme, including a handful of dessert tortillas.

La Fronda

C/Verdi 15, 08012 (93 415 30 57). Metro Fontana or Joanic. **Open** 8pm-12.30am Mon, Wed, Thur; 8pm-2.30am Fri, Sat; 8pm-12.30am Sun. Closed Aug. **Credit** V.

The wicker furniture, the leafy plants, the travel magazines; there is something very colonial about La Fronda. The wine list is very reasonably priced and there's a small selection of tapas, as well as excellent sandwiches, own-made cakes and ice-cream.

Gusto

C/Francisco Giner 24, 08012 (no phone). Metro Diagonal. **Open** 11pm-2.30am Wed-Sat. **No credit cards.**

A young crowd, a neat front bar where the DJ plays pre-club electronica, and a turquoise-lit back room that feels weirdly outdoors. The sand-strewn floor makes it either an indoor beach or a room-sized ashtray.

Snails baked a la llauna and monkfish stew are among the highlights at **El Glop** *p160* which has branches at **El Nou Glop** C/Montmany 49, torre (93 219 7059).

Gràcia

Mond Bar

C/Plaça del Sol, 08012 (607 310 015). Metro Diagonal.
Open 8.30pm-2.30am Mon-Thur, Sun; 8.30pm-3am Fri,
Sat. **No credit cards**.

Over a footbridge from the main square, this diminutive
bar on the Plaça del Sol runs youth-team try-outs all week
for aspiring local DJs. The ambience is cliquey and in-
the-know, with the emphasis on the offbeat fashion move
and the recondite but spot-on musical reference.

Mos

*Via Augusta 112, 08006 (93 237 13 13). FCG Plaça
Molina.* **Open** 7am-10pm Mon-Sat; 7.30am-10pm Sun.
Credit MC, V.

Oh, that all self-service cafés were as good as this! From
the tempting trays of hot and cold dishes that owe
nothing to canteen cuisine, to the delectable desserts and
even handmade chocolates; just point at what you want.
Food is weighed, marked on a ticket, you take it to the
café at the back, help yourself to drinks, then later tell
the staff what you've eaten. A smartly designed, elegant
space that is open 365 days of the year.

Gràcia

Salambó. *See p172.*

places for...

intimate dates

Cafè de l'Acadèmia (*see p27*), **Dry Martini** (*see p148*), **Mastroqué** (*see p33*), **Octubre** (*see p161*), **Ot** (*see p161*), **El Pebre Blau** (*see p105*), **Pla** (*see p37*), **La Reina** (*see p106*), **Semproniana** (*see p136*).

Salambó

C/Torrijos 51, 08012 (93 218 69 66). Metro Joanic.
Open noon-2.30am daily. **Credit** V.
By day, this is a large, sophisticated, split-level café serving coffee, teas and a good-value menú del dia to the barri's more conservative element. By night, it's not exactly revolutionary, but the music goes up loud and crowds from the Verdi cinema next door give it some life.

Sol Soler

Plaça del Sol 21, 08012 (93 217 44 40). Metro Fontana.
Open *May-Sept* noon-2am Mon-Thur; noon-3am Fri, Sat; noon-2am Sun. *Oct-Apr* 4pm-2am Mon-Wed; 3pm-2am Thur; 2pm-3am Fri; noon-3am Sat; noon-2am Sun.
No credit cards.
Sol Soler's nod towards stylish design – plenty of mirrors, wood-lined walls, bistro lighting – contrasts with the student caff feel given to it by having too many tables and noisy graciencs on a Saturday night. They come to taste the inventive salads (like tropical or Korean) and the roquefort quiche.

Sureny

Plaça Revolució 17, 08012 (93 213 75 56). Metro Joanic.
Open 8pm-1.30am Tue-Sun. **No credit cards**.
What Sureny lacks in the character of its brightly lit and bland decor, it more than makes up for in the quality of its gourmet tapas. As well as the run-of-the-mill varieties, the young but assured crowd comes for treats such as foie gras with mango and wine, or prawn and wild mushroom ravioli.

Virreina Bar

Plaça de la Virreina 1, 08024 (93 237 98 80). Metro Fontana. **Open** 10am-2.30am Mon-Sat; 10am-midnight Sun. **No credit cards**.
It's not that the inside of this place is bad (simple, vaguely alternative café with noticeboard of local happenings), it's just that the good bocadillos and imported beers taste even better when you're sitting outside in the tranquil square.

Ports & Shoreline

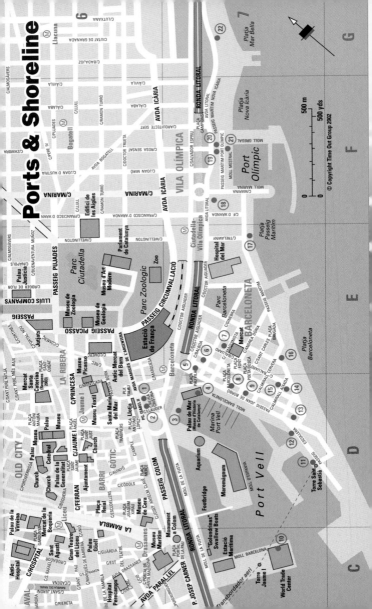

Restaurants

Agua ★

Passeig Marítim de la Barceloneta 30, 08003 (93 225 12 72). Metro Barceloneta. **Meals served** 1.30-4pm, 8.30pm-midnight Mon-Thur, Sun; 1.30-4pm, 8.30pm-1am Fri, Sat. **Average** €€. **Credit** AmEx, MC, V.

Another hit restaurant from the Tragaluz group, this one sits at the very edge of the beach, with unobstructed views from the terrace. The decor has an arty feel, with huge global village (beautiful children from far-off lands) prints on the walls, squidgy sofas and newspapers to keep you entertained while you wait. The crowd is generally young and informal. House specialities include arroz al carbón, fresh fish and seafood tapas, but the steaks and carpaccios can also be good. Booking is essential for Sunday lunch.

Agua

Can Ramonet

Can Majó

*C/Almirall Aixada 23, 08003 (93 221 54 55/
93 221 58 18). Metro Barceloneta.* **Meals served** 1-4pm,
8-11.30pm Tue-Sat; 1-4pm Sun. **Average** €€.
Credit AmEx, DC, MC, V.
One of the best of the dozens of seafood restaurants in
the area, Can Majó avoids the nautical trappings so
beloved of such places, with a smart, clean atmosphere
and cream and green walls. Start by sharing a 'pica-
pica' plate of shellfish, then move on to one of the
restaurant's excellent paellas or fideuàs. Fish is also
expertly prepared; cod comes with clams and salsa
verde (made with garlic and parsley) and the suquet is
a triumph: a sizzling panful of monkfish, hake, mussels,
clams, prawns and potatoes. Service, at worst, is
endearingly forgetful.

Can Maño

C/Baluard 12, 08003 (93 319 30 82). Metro Barceloneta.
Meals served 8am-11am, noon-4pm, 8-10.30pm Mon-Fri;
8am-4pm Sat. **Average** €. **No credit cards**.
Enjoy big, steaming plates of freshly caught seafood in
a restaurant that's always rowdy and packed to the gills
with locals. The friendly waiters reel off the daily
specials at lightning speed, but the best thing to choose

is nearly always the soft, creamy sepia (cuttlefish) cooked in garlic and parsley. At Can Maño there are chips with everything and a big doorstop of watermelon for dessert.

Can Ramonet

C/Maquinista 17, 08003 (93 319 30 64). Metro Barceloneta. **Meals served** 10am-4pm, 8pm-midnight Mon-Sat. Closed 2wks Jan, 2wks Aug. **Average** €€. **Credit** AmEx, DC, MC, V.

This quaint, rose-coloured restaurant is an old favourite among uptown yuppies visiting downtown Barceloneta, usually for a good Sunday paella in the sunshine with all the family. Spectacular displays of fresh seafood show what's on offer that day, and you can either have a full menu or just sit around the giant wooden barrels to nibble some traditional seafood tapas.

Can Solé ★

C/Sant Carles 4, 08003 (93 221 50 12). Metro Barceloneta. **Meals served** 1.30-4pm, 8-11pm Tue-Sat; 1.30-4pm Sun. Closed 2wks Aug. **Average** €€€. **Credit** AmEx, DC, MC, V.

Can Solé opened in 1903, and occupies a charming building decorated with glazed tiles which tell the story of the restaurant in pictures and rhyming couplets. It is

Choreographies

Dancers with torches
& fire-eaters

Shows with water

Live Songs

Coyote Shots

The most cosmopolitan
atmosphere in the city

The craziest parties

The show never ends

COYOTE
UGLY

How to get there: Av. del Litoral 24
(next to Torre Mapfre)

Zone Puerto Olímpico

Metro: Ciutadella Vila Olímpica L4

Buses: 41-36-N0-N6-N8

Open from Thursday to Saturday from midnight until 5 am
In summer open from 11:30 pm until 5 am, also on Wednesdays.

Sponsors: Budweiser BACARDI Dewar's White Label

just 5m off the main tourist drag – a small step for the customer but a giant leap for paella. Arroz a la paella Parellada is dark and delicious with the rice crisped up around the edges, and spiked with the juiciest seafood imaginable. This and many other paellas and fideuàs are joined by a host of delights such as monkfish soup, lobster stew, tiny wild octopus, Palamòs prawns, the freshest fish, and every crustacean served to the peak of perfection. The scumbled, sea-blue walls heave with awards, photos and mementoes of regular customers (including Joan Miró and Santiago Rusiñol), while the bustle of the open kitchen works well with Can Solé's friendly atmosphere.

Newport Room

Hotel Arts, C/Marina 19-21, 08005 (93 221 10 00). Metro Ciutadella-Vila Olímpica. **Meals served** 7.30-11.30pm daily. **Average** €€€€. **Credit** AmEx, DC, MC, V.

The newly refurbished star restaurant of the monumental Hotel Arts, with unrivalled views of the sea and Frank Gehry's wonderful bronze fish sculpture. The knowledgeable but unstuffy service complements the internationally influenced, gourmet cuisine, which must be only a heartbeat away from earning American chef Toni Bombaci his first Michelin star. Try generous shavings of white truffles and pasta, duck breast with tissue-thin bacon and date paste, or leek soup over creamy foie gras ice-cream. All the ingredients are superlatively fresh and often locally produced, while the wine selection is everything you would hope for in a restaurant of this quality.

El Rebujito de Moncho's

C/Marina 16, local 10, 08005 (93 221 38 83). Metro Ciutadella-Vila Olímpica. **Meals served** noon-midnight daily. **Average** €. **Credit** AmEx, MC, V.

Not the most atmospheric of restaurants, but certainly the most affordable on this strip, with a well-priced all-you-can-eat buffet. The food on offer includes pasta, paella, chicken and a couple of fish dishes, with plenty of salads. To get away from the coach parties – or at least have something else to look at – sit out on the terrace and watch the boats in the harbour.

A branch of paella specialist **Elche** *p197* can be found at **L'Elche al Moll**, Maremàgnum, Moll d'Espanya, Port Vell, 08039 (93 225 8117).

Ruccula

World Trade Center, Moll de Barcelona, 08039 (93 508 82 68). Metro Drassanes. **Meals served** 1-4pm, 8.30pm-midnight Mon-Sat; 1-4pm Sun. **Average** €€. **Credit** AmEx, DC, MC, V.

Ruccula has so successfully blended traditional and modern that on our visit a lavatory assistant was dressed in a French maid's outfit and reading the share prices in the newspaper. The restaurant's stark brown and grey decor, largely business clientele and location in the WTC (albeit with great views over the port) make for staid surroundings and give no hint at the delights that emerge from the kitchen. A large, creamy portion of besugo (sea bream) with wedge clams and peppercorns and a rich, flavoursome monkfish and potato suquet are just two of the luxuries on offer. Rice dishes, too, are excellent – try partridge and artichoke risotto, but leave room for the desserts. On a good day, they might include a coulant (like a soufflé, but runny in the middle) of Idiazàbal cheese with membrillo and walnut ice-cream.

Salamanca

C/Almirante Cervera 34, 08003 (93 221 50 33). Metro Barceloneta. **Meals served** 10am-1am daily. **Average** €€. **Credit** AmEx, DC, MC, V.

With a huge and lively terrace yards from the beach and a warren of packed and rowdy dining rooms, Salamanca is not the place for an intimate meal. The service is utterly haphazard and starters and main courses arrive in a jumble. It's not a bad place to take kids, however, who just blend in with the general chaos and are looked after with a rare children's menu. Stick with the shellfish here – the paella and fideuà are produced in such vast quantities that they lack a certain finesse. Another, perhaps surprising, speciality comes in the form of cochinillo, suckling pig, tender roasted and served with little green peppers.

Set Portes ★

Passeig d'Isabel II 14, 08003 (93 319 30 33/ 93 319 29 50/ www.7puertas.com). Metro Barceloneta. **Meals served** 1pm-1am daily. **Average** €€. **Credit** AmEx, DC, MC, V.

Founded in 1836, the gigantic 'Seven Doors' has reached the status of an institution. It is, without doubt, Barcelona's most famous temple to paella, and there is always a queue of hungry pilgrims outside at lunchtime and in the evening. Despite its popularity, Set Portes has managed to maintain the quality of its seafood and rice dishes, although the vastness of the place can be off-putting, as can the house pianist playing 'Three Times a Lady' on the baby grand. The waiters and maître d' are fabulously accommodating and the most stubborn of non-linguists will be coaxed through the menu.

Suquet de l'Almirall ★

Passeig de Joan de Borbó 65, 08003 (93 221 62 33). Metro Barceloneta. **Meals served** 1-4pm, 9-11pm Tue-Sat; 1-4pm Sun. **Average** €€. **Credit** AmEx, DC, MC, V.

A cut above the other restaurants along this seaside strip, Suquet de l'Almirall's reputation for excellent seafood makes reservations essential, especially at lunchtime.

Can Solé. See p177.

There is a pretty terrace but it's almost a shame to miss the cosy ochre and yellow interior decorated with aquarelles of wonderfully po-faced fish. (The brick-lined basement room is less attractive.) The best way to eat here is to try one of the set menus, which include a seven-course sampler, the 'blind menu' of seven tapas and a rice dish, or the light pica-pica with tomato coca bread, red pepper escalivada with anchovies, battered cod croquettes, fried fish, a huge bowl of steamed shellfish, rock-salted king prawns, and a knockout fideuà of noodles and lobster.

Talaia Mar

C/Marina 16, 08005 (93 221 90 90/www.talaia-mar.es). Metro Ciutadella-Vila Olímpica. **Meals served** 1-4pm, 8pm-midnight daily. **Average** €€€. **Credit** AmEx, DC, MC, V.

Food festivals

Gastronomic festivals, where a particular food type is celebrated in season in the town or region best known for it, abound throughout Catalonia. The following is just a small selection; for more information about food festivals contact your local tourist office.

Calçots

La Gran Festa de la Calçotada (Valls, last Sunday of January). Char-grilled in vast quantities on a blazing open fire and dipped in romesco sauce, these long spring onions (pictured, right) are as much a social phenomenon as a regional foodstuff. The season starts with free calçot tastings in one of the best gastronomic festivals in Catalonia.

Sea urchins

La Garoinada (Palafrugell, mid January to mid March). The best spot and season to try these spiky creatures (garoines or garotes in Catalan), usually cut open and eaten raw with a spoon. Offered free in the market or bought at stands near the beach.

Xató

La Ruta del Xató (coast south of Barcelona, late January to March). A salad with escarole lettuce, salt cod, tuna and anchovies, with a sauce of peppers (nyores), nuts and garlic, xató is a lenten dish found where carnival is most celebrated. The 'xatonades' starts in Sitges the week

---

Ports & Shoreline

Talaia Mar has had a couple of exciting chefs in recent times and consequently enjoys a reputation for cutting edge, new wave Catalan cooking. We were faintly disappointed, then, when the parade of dishes – calçot (Catalan onion) tempura, wild mushroom cannelloni, red mullet and Moroccan lamb – marched across the table without incident, unless you count the nube de soja (a 'cloud' of soy foam) accompanying the tempura. The 'festival gastronómico', a nine-course feast for €55, might have proved less predictable. It's all competently prepared and presented, however, and the sleek design and rounded glass front looking over the harbour make this a glorious spot for lunch.

Torre de Altamar

Passeig deJoan de Borbó 88, 08003 (93 221 0007). Metro Jaume I. **Meals served** 8.30-11.30pm Mon; 1-3.30pm, 8.30-11.30pm Tue-Sat. **Average** €€€€. **Credit** AmEx, MC, V.

Spiked on the top of the cablecar tower, at the summit of a dizzying 75m lift ride, this new and wildly fashionable restaurant has spectacular views; try to get a table on the

before carnival and moves to Vilanova i la Geltrú on the second Sunday of February.

Prawns

El Menú de la Gamba (Palamòs, late April to late June). The finest Mediterranean prawns, served in top Barcelona restaurants. Promoted in specially prepared dishes in various restaurants of this Costa Brava town.

Snails

Aplec del Cargol (Lleida, three days in mid May). Catalonia's most visited food festival, held in a beech grove across the river from the city. Scores of local clubs set up their own stands with snail recipes.

Bull

El Berenar del Bou (Amposta, mid August). A huge free tasting of stewed bull meat, from fighting bulls that run through the town streets.

Funghi

Festa dels Bolets (Berga, first weekend of October). A picking contest, competitive gastronomy and mycology exhibitions, and tastings on the Sunday.

city side for the full effect. The decor assimilates all that is currently hip – Shanghai Lil and Twiggy do Bladerunner – but the steeply priced food, a fairly limited selection of fish and seafood, is not always so impressive, and not quite as fresh as one might expect from a restaurant suspended above the sea. The average customer – a mobile-wielding uptowner – appears not to notice that the food could be better or that the view could not. Torre de Altamar is a once in a lifetime experience, but probably best kept that way.

Xiringuitó Escribà

Litoral Mar 42 (Platja Bogatell), 08005 (93 221 07 29). Metro Ciutadella-Vila Olímpica. **Meals served** *Oct-Mar* 11am-4.30pm Tue-Sun. *Apr, May* 11am-4.30pm Tue-Thur; 11am-4.30pm, 9-11.30pm Fri, Sat; 10.30am-5.15pm Sun. *June-Sept* 11am-4.30pm, 9-11.30pm Mon-Sat; 10.30am-5.15pm Sun. **Average** €€€. **Credit** MC, V.

There is one thing you should know about Xiringuitó Escribà straight off: the service is execrable. If you're not in a hurry, however, you have a treat in store: the restaurant is smack on the beach, but away from the

Can Paixano

tourist drag, and the food is excellent. The specialities are
rice dishes and fideuà, but with such wonderful starters
– a warm salad with tender partridge escabeche, for
example, or young artichokes with scallops and baby
broad beans – having two is not a bad option. The
Escribàs are a well-known pastry-making dynasty, and
the desserts are reputedly spectacular. We wouldn't know
– after waiting for an hour, we gave up and got the bill.

International

dZI

Passeig de Joan de Borbó 76, 08003 (93 221 21 82).
Metro Barceloneta. **Meals served** 1-4pm, 8pm-midnight
daily. **Average** €€. **Credit** AmEx, MC, V.
dZI's healthy and light pan-Asian cuisine offers a change
from seafood. Service is polite, and dishes have little in
common with the MSG-laden salt licks that pass for food

in Barcelona's cheaper Asian restaurants. Try chicken with black mushrooms, water chestnuts and rice baked in a banana leaf, green curry soup or spicy tiger prawns while enjoying the view of the port from the shady terrace.

Cafés & Bars

Port Olímpic has a line of bars with little to choose between them, unless go-go dancers and the latest cheesy hits are your thing.

Café & Café

Moll del Mestral 30, 08005 (93 221 00 19). Metro Ciutadella-Vila Olímpica. **Open** 3pm-3am Mon-Thur; 4pm-5am Fri, Sat; noon-3am Sun. **Credit** AmEx, DC, MC, V.
An oasis of calm on this noisy strip, this café-cum-cocktail bar has a mind-boggling range of coffees, often combined with alcohol.

Can Ganassa

Plaça de la Barceloneta 4-6, 08003 (93 225 19 97). Metro Barceloneta. **Open** *June-Sept* 9-1.30am Mon, Tue, Thur-Sun. *Oct-May* 9am-11pm Mon, Tue, Thur-Sun. **No credit cards.**
It's smoky, it's noisy, it's full of gruff old men competing to be heard above the fruit machines – we love it. And besides, there are tables outside. Great tapas are nearly all on display, so you don't need to worry about flexing your Catalan, just point. Try the bomba Ganassa, a potato and bacon croquette served with all i oli and a fiery chilli sauce.

Can Paixano

C/Reina Cristina 7, 08003 (93 310 08 39). Metro Barceloneta. **Meals served** 9am-10.30pm Mon-Sat. **No credit cards.**
You'll need to master the art of elbowing and sidling at this standing-room only bodega, known as the 'champagne bar'. Cava flows liberally at all hours, accompanied by dirt-cheap bocadillos. It has no sign and is buried among cheap electronics shops; just follow the sound of the hubbub.

Jai-ca

C/Ginebra 13, 08003 (93 319 50 02). Metro Barceloneta. **Meals served** 10am-midnight daily. **Credit** MC, V.
The jumble of tables in the tight space inside this no-nonsense tapas bar spills out on to a pleasant, shaded terrace. Its location on the corner of two quiet streets, with a fresh breeze wafting through and a permanently stopped clock on the wall make for a lazy, informal atmosphere. It's a perfect pre- or post-beach stop-off.

Branches of **Hostal El Pintor** *p31* are located at **Mandongo,** Maremagnum, Local 108, 08039, Port Vell (93 225 81 43); **Travi Mar,** Maremagnum, Local 110, 08039, Port Vell (93 225 81 36).

Ports & Shoreline

El Vaso de Oro

Luz de Gas – Port Vell

Opposite the Palau de Mar, 08003 (93 209 77 11/
www.luzdegas.com). Metro Barceloneta or Jaume I.
Meals served noon-3am Mon-Fri; 11am-3am Sun.
Closed Nov-Feb. **Credit** AmEx, MC, V.
This floating two-deck bar is docked in the Port Vell
alongside a promenade buzzing with Rollerbladers, cyclers
and strollers. At nightfall, candles are brought out, wine
is uncorked and the scene acquires an air of romance,
marred only by the cheesy music.

La Miranda del Museu ★

Museu d'Història de Catalunya, Plaça Pau Vila 1, 08003
(93 225 50 07). Metro Barceloneta. **Meals served** 10am-
7pm Tue-Sat. **Credit** MC, V.
In a city known for its wonderful views, this top-floor café
has one of the best, especially as the sun sinks down behind
Montjuïc, bathing the city in a lustrous orange glow. The
enormous terrace is perfect for young children to let off
steam, and there is also a great-value set lunch. You don't
need a museum ticket; just take the lift to the top floor.

El Vaso de Oro

C/Balboa 6, 08003 (93 319 30 98). Metro Barceloneta.
Meals served 9am-midnight daily. Closed Sept.
No credit cards.
The charm lies in the decor – like a bar on a down-at-heel
1950s cruise ship with liveried staff, cramped layout and
dark wooden fittings. It's always noisy and bustling and
has some of the best tapas in town; especially good are the
patatas bravas. Get there early for a seat in the wings.

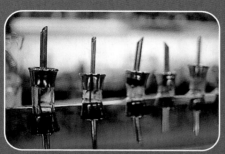

Zona Alta

Restaurants

La Balsa ★

*C/Infanta Isabel 4, 08022 (93 211 50 48). FCG Av
Tibidabo.* **Meals served** 9-11.30pm Mon; 2-3.30pm, 9-
11.30pm Tue-Sat. **Average** €€€. **Credit** AmEx, MC, V.
The grand location among the mansions of high society;
the sniffy parking attendant, the glorious award-winning
building among lush gardens ablaze with geraniums: all
of this might lead you to expect fancy forkfuls of minimal
food. Not so. The menu, like the restaurant, has a country
feel to it, and is more likely to feature escudella (Catalan
winter stew) or cabbage leaves stuffed with partridge
than itsy-bitsy polenta bites. The portions are enormous;
a starter of trinxat de verdures, a vegetable bubble-and-
squeak, came laden with ham and fried egg and could
easily have fed a family, while duck magret covered a
whole plate. On cold winter nights, a log fire crackles,
while in summer there can be nowhere as pretty as the
verdant, jasmine-scented terrace.

Neichel ★

*C/Beltrán i Rózpide 16 bis, 08034 (93 203 84 08). Metro
Maria Cristina.* **Meals served** 1-3.30pm, 8.30-11.30pm
Tue-Sat. Closed Aug. **Average** €€€€. **Credit** AmEx,
DC, MC, V.
With a quiet location in the smart part of town, Neichel
has established a sterling reputation for excellent food
and wine. Alsace-born Jean-Louis Neichel creates
elaborate variants on classic Mediterranean and French
dishes, inspired by his native and adoptive countries. The
extensive menu features a menú degustación, another of
five truffle dishes, and several daily suggestions. To start,
prawns with wild mushrooms were velvety and divine.
Delicious spoonfuls of lobster and prawn tartar came in
a blaze of marine and vegetable life, including baby eels
and asparagus. The main courses were equally good;
venison with rhubarb and fruits of the forest was
satisfyingly gamey, a taste offset by various citric
flavours. Servings are generous, so take care if you want
to make the most of the fantastic cheese and dessert
trolleys. The atmosphere is somewhat staid, the service
somewhat tardy.

St Rémy

C/Iradier 12, 08017 (93 418 75 04). FCG Sarrià. **Meals
served** 1-3.30pm, 8-11pm Mon-Sat; 1-3.30pm Sun.
Average €€. **Credit** AmEx, DC, MC, V.
Set in the spacious covered interior of what was once the
garden courtyard of a Sarrià townhouse, St Rémy has
become a reliable favourite for uptown diners. The

Zona Alta

internationalised Catalan menu features sprightly seafood salads for starters, with main courses of lamb and veal, carpaccio variations, or an excellent choice of baked fish, which varies according to the season. The presentation is attractive, though the sheer size of the usually packed place makes for uninterested service and a certain impersonal quality that affects both the ambience and the food itself. Advance booking is essential.

Tram-Tram

C/Major de Sarrià 121, 08017 (93 204 85 18). FCG
Reina Elisenda. **Meals served** 9-11pm Mon; 1.30-3.30pm,
9-11pm Tue-Fri; 9-11pm Sat. Closed 2wks Aug. **Average**
€€€. **Credit** AmEx, DC, MC, V.
Through a couple of quiet and rather plain dining rooms
lies Tram-Tram's hidden gem: a pretty little garden
terrace. Elsewhere the heavy oil still-lifes dotted around

A branch of glorious light-filled **Tragaluz** *p136* can be found at **Acontraluz** C/Milanesat 19, Zona Alta (93 203 0658).

La Venta

the walls prelude the huntin', shootin' and fishin' nature of the menu. Rich and elaborate dishes change with the season, but game from hare to venison often features, and foie gras appears in many guises. There is also a short list of 'classic' dishes, including sardines with baby vegetables and buffalo mozzarella on coca (Catalan flat, crispy bread), and courgette millefeuille with goat's cheese and black olives. An excellent wine list is particularly strong on Spanish reds, and there is a lengthy menú degustación. The lunchtime menu at €18 is more functional than gastronomically interesting.

La Venta ★

Plaça Doctor Andreu 1, 08035 (93 212 64 55). FCG Av Tibidabo, then Tramvia Blau. **Meals served** 1.30-3.15pm, 9-11.15pm Mon-Sat. **Average** €€€. **Credit** AmEx, DC, MC, V.

La Venta serves excellent modern Spanish cuisine in a lovely setting, perched high above Barcelona. The rambling building, set in the square below the Tibidabo cable car, has outdoor terraces and a glassed-in conservatory that create an airy, out of the city feel. Starters include delicacies such as erizos de mar gratinados (sea urchins au gratin) and delicious salads – baby broad bean and fresh mozzarella is particularly good. Steaks are available in huge or sensibly moderate sizes, the rack of lamb is a speciality and great fish choices include delicate monkfish wrapped in filo pastry with pesto and tomato coulis. Many of the creative desserts feature superb seasonal fruits. Smart Barcelona families converge on La Venta on weekends, so book ahead.

Vivanda

C/Major de Sarrià 134, 08017 (93 205 47 17). Metro FCG Reina Elisenda. **Meals served** 9-11.30pm Mon; 1-3.30pm, 9-11.30pm Tue-Sat. **Average** €€. **Credit** DC, MC, V.
Located in an older townhouse in the quaint part of historical Sarrià, Vivanda's remodelled dining room and airy back garden terrace enhance its relaxed and unpretentious ambience. The food here is equally unassuming: a bit nouvelle, a bit conventional, generally well prepared and served by a warm and attentive staff. Starters include fish soup, shellfish salads and seasonally fresh vegetables, while the main courses featured are grilled monkfish, hake or tuna with light, creative sauces and, usually, a couple of foie options. The reliable approach to cooking is followed through in Catalan standards such as botifarra, veal and duck, as well as seasonal game. There is also an excellent value set lunch at €9.

International

Ken

C/Benet i Mateu 53, 08034 (93 203 20 44). FGC Les Tres Torres. **Meals served** 1.30-4pm Mon; 8.30pm-midnight Tue-Sun. Closed Aug. **Average** €€. **Credit** MC, V.
Be sure to book a seat at the counter for a show of dazzling culinary theatre in this Japanese restaurant specialising in a la plancha dishes. The planchas in question are two wide griddles that become the stage for a performance of frying, tossing, chopping, teasing and effortless artistry. There are sushi, sashimi and tempura dishes on offer, all beautifully prepared and presented, but the real speciality here is seafood: clams, scallops, langoustines and squid. For the undecided, there are three set menus comprising fish, meat and noodle dishes.

Sophisticated Catalan cooking is on offer at **Les Quinze Nits** *p38* and its branch **L'Hostalet de la Mamasita** Avda Sarrià 10, 08029, Zona Alta (93 321 9296).

Gimlet

Cafés & Bars

Bar Tomás

*C/Major de Sarrià 49, 08017 (93 203 10 77). FGC
Sarrià.* **Open** 7.45am-10pm Mon, Tue, Thur-Sun.
No credit cards.
Every now and then a foodstuff will assume iconic
status; just as pa amb tomàquet is a symbol of
Catalonia, Bar Tomás's patatas bravas have become the
emblematic tapa for Barcelona. Whether they merit the
schlep across town or the queues on Sunday is
irrelevant; until you've tried them, your Barcelona
experience is incomplete.

Gimlet

C/Santaló 46, 08021 (93 201 53 06). FGC Muntaner.
Open 7pm-3am daily. **Credit** MC, V.
With its black bar, red stools and predominance of
straight lines, there's something very '80s about this
friendly bar. Despite this, Gimlet has never really gone
out of style for those looking for a well-mixed cocktail.
There's also a terrace for the summer months where you
can watch all the beautiful uptown people.

The best view

Mirablau
(see below).

La Miranda del Museu
(see p186).

Talaia Mar
(see p181).

Torre de Altamar
(see p182).

La Venta
(see p191).

Merbeyé

Plaça Doctor Andreu, 08035 (93 417 92 79). FGC Av Tibidabo, then Tramvia Blau/60 bus. **Open** noon-2.30am Mon-Thur, Sun; noon-3.30am Fri, Sat. **Credit** MC, V.

If Humphrey Bogart had a cocktail bar, it would be something like this, bedecked in red velvet with monochrome prints of jazz luminaries on the walls, low lighting and a peaceful, stylish terrace. Later on, the crowd – Barça team members and the like – crosses to the late night disco in Mirablau.

Mirablau

Plaça Doctor Andreu, 08035 (93 418 58 79). FGC Av Tibidabo, then Tramvia Blau/60 bus. **Open** 11am-4.30am Mon-Thur, Sun; 11am-5am Fri, Sat. **Credit** MC, V.

At the foot of the Tibidabo funicular, Mirablau has floor-to-ceiling windows with spectacular views. At night, the flash cars outside attest to its status as playground for the international set (there's a dancefloor downstairs), but in the day it's an approachable, if pricey, bar with good bocadillos, toasted sandwiches and a terrace.

Partycular

Avda Tibidabo 61, 08035 (93 211 62 61/www.partycular. com). FGC Av Tibidabo. **Open** 7pm-3am Wed-Sun. **Credit** MC, V.

Partycular is a pleasure dome in a three-storey mansion on the way up to Tibidabo. Blue-carpeted steps welcome a well-heeled international crowd to the plush bar and restaurant. The gardens and terraces that spill downhill, dotted with bars and secluded areas, are ideal for relaxing in summer.

Lavinia (Avda Diagonal 605) is Barcelona's newest, biggest and best wine shop, with a staggering selection of wine from every corner of the globe, and some interesting organic choices.

Zona Alta

Poble Sec & Sants

Restaurants

La Bodegueta

C/Blai 47, 08004 (93 442 08 46). Metro Poble Sec. **Meals served** 1.30-4pm, 8.30pm-midnight Tue-Sun. Closed 2wks Aug. **Average** €. **Credit** MC, V.

Another wonderful old bodega-turned-restaurant, with oak barrels of wine, sherry and anis stacked up the walls, and gruff but affable waiters. Hunks of pa amb tomàquet (*see p57*) accompanied by plates of anchovies, tuna, smoked salmon, jamón iberico and cabrales cheese are the main event here, but there are also great a la brasa dishes: entrecôte, rabbit, pork and lamb cutlets.

Elche

C/Vilà i Vilà 71, 08004 (93 441 30 89). Metro Paral.lel. **Meals served** 12.45-4.30pm, 8pm-midnight Mon-Fri; 1pm-12.30am Sat; 1pm-midnight Sun. **Average** €€. **Credit** AmEx, MC, V.

Originally run by two brothers (one now runs the sister restaurant in Maremàgnum) who still make use of their mother's recipes, Elche specialises in all types of paellas and fideuàs. The starters (which can be had in half-portions) are delectable; try the peppers stuffed with cream of monkfish. The split-level restaurant is slightly lacking in character, however, and the piped music doesn't really help.

La Parra.
See p198.

Taverna Can Margarit

La Opalina

C/Riego 25, 08014 (93 421 84 74). Metro Plaça de Sants or Sants Estació. **Meals served** 1-4pm Mon, Sun; 1-4pm, 9pm-midnight Tue-Sat. **Average** €€. **No credit cards**.

Five minutes' walk from Sants train station, this low-ceilinged, brightly coloured restaurant is an agreeable place to grab a cheap bite before your train leaves. The set lunch menu is good value and might feature llenguado (sole) with an almond sauce, or spare ribs with all i oli, although desserts can be a bit dreary. There's also a slightly pricier set menu with an emphasis on inventive cod dishes.

La Parra ★

C/Joanot Martorell 3, 08014 (93 332 51 34).
Metro Hostafrancs. **Meals served** 8.30pm-12.30am Tue-Fri; 2-4.30pm, 8.30pm-midnight Sat; 2-4.30pm Sun. Closed Aug. **Average** €€. **Credit** MC, V.

This 19th-century coaching inn now houses one of the city's best restaurants for Catalan a la brasa cooking. Boulders of meat, still spitting from the fierce wood-fired grill, are served on slabs of wood and accompanied by ferociously strong all i oli. Lamb (actually mutton, and none the worse for it) is served alongside goat, horse, beef and rabbit, but the tastiest dish might just be the succulent galtes (pig's cheeks). The cosy and traditionally decorated interior is the perfect place to be on a cold winter's night, while in summer the eponymous vine provides cool shade on the peaceful terrace.

Poble Sec & Sants

Peixerot ★

C/Tarragona 177, 08014 (93 424 69 69). Metro Sants Estació. **Meals served** *Jan-July, Sept-Dec* 1-4pm, 8.30-11pm Mon-Sat; 1-4pm Sun. *Aug* 1-4pm, 8.30-11pm Mon-Fri; 1-4pm Sat. **Average** €€€. **Credit** AmEx, DC, MC, V.

Peixerot's noisy, animated dining room is draped and ruched à la wedding reception, with squadrons of smart white-jacketed waiters ready to take your order. Although some of the fixtures and fittings are a little battered now, it's hard to care in the face of such excellent and consistent cooking. Order your food by weight and choose from a host of different ways to have it cooked: baked inside a wet salt envelope, a la marinera with tomato and onion, fried, grilled or San Sebastian style with garlic, hot peppers and vinegar. House specialities here are the superlative xató de Vilanova salad with cod and anchovies, and paellas with the juiciest, fluffiest lobster, recently plucked from an Olympic-sized tank.

Taverna Can Margarit

C/Concòrdia 21, 08004 (93 441 67 23). Metro Poble Sec. **Meals served** 9-11.30pm Mon-Thur; 9-11.45pm Fri, Sat. Closed Aug. **Average** €. **Credit** MC, V.

The huge kegs piled high in this 200-year-old barn-like building are a reminder of its original activity as a wine distribution point for the whole of Barcelona. Now a popular restaurant, it's an easy-going place; Enric will encourage you to help yourself to wine from a barrel while you wait for a table. The house speciality, conill a la Jumillana (a tasty rabbit concoction served with onions and garlic), is the highlight of a traditional menu. The rest of the classic Catalan fare (grilled meats, escalivada and botifarra) can be rather blandly done. Taverna Can Margarit isn't the place for a low-key, intimate evening, as the frequent birthday parties can get pretty noisy

La Tomaquera

C/Margarit 58, 08004 (no phone). Metro Paral.lel. **Meals served** 1.30-4pm, 8.30-11.30pm Tue-Sat. Closed Aug. **Average** €. **No credit cards**.

From the moment you enter the world of red gingham and bright lighting that is La Tomaquera, staff will bark imperious instructions at you, many of which are reproduced in detail on the walls. There will be no booking, there is no telephone, there is only house wine, there is only a brasa meat – and if you don't like it, you can go elsewhere. Judging by the lack of empty tables, Barcelonins obviously do like it, for they come in droves to tuck into huge portions of perfectly cooked meat served with weapons-grade all i oli.

El Celler de Gélida (C/Vallespir 65) is an excellently stocked wine shop with knowledgeable staff, just off the Plaça de Sants.

International

La Bella Napoli

C/Margarit 14, 08004 (93 442 50 56). Metro Paral.lel.
Meals served 1.30-4pm, 8.30pm-midnight Tue-Sun.
Average €. **Credit** DC, MC, V.

A traditional wood-burning pizza oven presides over this restaurant like steaming Vesuvius over namesake Naples. The pleasant, smiling Neapolitan staff take pride in the authenticity of the generous menu, which features antipasti – try the arancino (fried rice and cheese), or the melanzane (sizzling aubergine slices) – followed by delicious thin-crust pizzas, pasta and meat scaloppina dishes. Many of the meat dishes come draped in mozzarella or provolone; a lighter more adventurous choice is the swordfish carpaccio. All the desserts, like the rich cassata siciliana, are own-made, and there is a strong selection of wines from all over Italy.

Cafés & Bars

Barcelona Rouge

C/Poeta Cabanyes 21, 08004 (93 442 49 85). Metro Paral.lel. **Open** 11pm-4am Tue-Sat. **Credit** MC, V.

Olives in Catalonia

In Catalonia eating olives is a matter of personal taste, but cooking with olive oil is a basic cultural tenet. To eat out in Barcelona is to consume it, as it is routinely used to sauté, dress and dip. Its non-saturated fats are cholesterol-free and are said to be behind Mediterranean longevity.

There are four grades of Spanish olive oil, and the best is virgin, the pure, first pressing – formerly done with a stone and now mechanised – which at its best has a very low acidity level. Overly acidic virgin pressings are often 'refined', making the second grade, and mixed with virgin to get the standard oil – the third grade, called simply 'olive oil'. It is this that is bottled by major producers such as Borges in Catalonia and Carbonell in Andalucia. The low-grade pomace oil (aceite de orujo in Spanish) processed from leftover pulp, is a thin, tasteless version used for deep frying.

As with official wine districts, Catalonia has two olive oil denominaciones de origen: Les Garrigues in Lleida and Siurana in Tarragona. The

Quimet i Quimet. *See p202.*

Quimet i Quimet. *See p202.*

2001 award for the finest quality oil in Spain went to a Siurana brand called Montebrione produced at Montbrió del Camp. Catalan oil is of such a high quality that much of the production is sold to Italian distributors, who bottle it as their own for export to their vaster world market.

A recent trend in eating olives is the wonderful tiny arbequina, traditionally the dominant Catalan variety used for oil. They now compete with the classic green manzanillas and other types native to Andalucia. No olive is edible unless pickled, something the EU agriculture commissioner, an Austrian, discovered after picking one off a Spanish tree and sticking it in his mouth, setting off a minor political incident. A standard pickling brine includes salt, garlic cloves and dill, although different combinations – hot peppers for added spiciness – are used. Another favourite eating version is called muertas (literally, dead), an overripe bluish-black version. Particularly good dry olives are the aragonesas muertas, the ominous 'dead Aragonese'.

Poble Sec & Sants

The buzzer in the cherub-encrusted doorway gives this place its clandestine feel. It's an intimate, offbeat, cocktail-sipping chill-out, with fuddled oil paintings, enigmatic murals and battered soft furnishings in the main bar. The music wriggles its way from outré to laid-back.

Bar Primavera

C/Nou de la Rambla 192, 08004 (93 329 30 62). Metro Paral.lel. **Open** *May-Oct* 8am-10pm Tue-Sun. *Nov-Apr* 8am-5pm Tue-Sun. **No credit cards**.
At the very end of C/Nou de la Rambla is this peaceful leafy terrace looking down on the city. There is no indoor seating, but shade is provided by vines overhead. With a small bar serving rudimentary bocadillos and snacks, this is the perfect place for a pit-stop on the climb up the hill.

Cervecería Jazz

C/Margarit 43, 08004 (93 443 32 59). Metro Paral.lel. **Open** 7pm-3am Mon-Sat. **No credit cards**.
Belgian beers, a long wooden bar and a rustic-meets-baroque interior make this an original bar. An earthenware jug holds olives and pickles, and good sandwiches are served. The music is mainly mixed jazz.

Fundació Joan Miró

Parc de Montjuic s/n, 08038 (93 329 07 68). Metro Espanya, then 50 bus. **Open** 10am-6.30pm Tue-Sat; 10am-2pm Sun. **Credit** MC, V.
This museum café (you don't need a ticket) is one of few decent places on Montjuïc. There are tables inside or you can sit in the grassy courtyard in the company of the artist's goblin ceramics. There's a choice of inventive sandwiches and more substantial dishes at lunchtime.

Quimet i Quimet ★

C/Poeta Cabanyes 25, 08004 (93 442 31 42). Metro Paral.lel. **Open** 7pm-3am Mon-Sat. **No credit cards**.
This is a popular bodega, with ceiling-high shelves stocked with wine, beer, liqueur and cava, ranging from bargain-basement to very upmarket. There are only three tables and nowhere to sit, but the tapas are excellent.

Tinta Roja

C/Creu dels Molers 17, 08004 (93 443 32 43). Metro Poble Sec. **Open** 5pm-1.30am Tue-Thur, Sun; 5pm-3am Fri, Sat. *Admission* €5 tango Sat. **No credit cards**.
The walls of this small, smoky bar are full of yellowing photos of tango shows and old Argentina, set off by dozens of 1960s and '70s-style dressing table mirrors and fairy lights. Deeper into the bar and you're pleasantly surprised by an avant-garde art exhibition that opens up to a theatre. There are tango lessons on Tuesdays and, occasionally, tango shows on Saturdays.

Poble Sec & Sants

Horta & Poblenou

Restaurants

Can Travi Nou

C/Jorge Manrique s/n, 08035 (93 428 03 01).
Metro Horta or Montbau. **Meals served** 1.30-4pm,
8.30pm-midnight Mon-Sat; 1.30-4pm Sun. **Average** €€€.
Credit AmEx, DC, MC, V.

In summer, diners sit on a vast covered terrace
surrounded by dense vegetation, seemingly a million
miles from the bustle of the city. In winter, the action (and
tables) move inside the huge, beautiful, old farmhouse,
perched on a hill above the former village of Horta. The
food is traditional Catalan, with speciality mar i
muntanya dishes, such as sípia amb mandonguilles
(squid with meatballs) and cueta de rap amb all torrat
(monkfish tail with toasted garlic) with great traditional
puddings, which come accompanied by a decanter of
dessert wine; just help yourself. Can Travi Nou is difficult
to reach by public transport – best to take a cab – but the
restaurant is very much worth seeking out.

Can Travi Nou

Can Travi Nou. *See p205*

Gaig ★

*Passeig Maragall 402, 08031 (93 429 10 17). Metro
Horta.* **Meals served** 1.30-4pm, 9-11pm Tue-Sat; 1.30-
4pm Sun. Closed 3wks Aug. **Average** €€€€.
Credit AmEx, DC, MC, V.

Carles Gaig, to whose family this restaurant has belonged
for 130 years, believes that more than three elements on
a plate is too many. But, oh, what elements! From the
crayfish tempura amuse-gueules, served with a dip of
creamed leek salted with pancetta, through to a shotglass
holding layers of tangy lemon syrup, crema catalana
mousse and caramel ice-cream topped with burned sugar
(to be eaten by plunging the spoon all the way down),
every dish is as surprising and perfectly composed as the
last. Order the degustación and the chef will discuss
anything you might like changed, but leave yourself in
his hands and you might be treated to oysters in an
impossibly creamy champagne sauce; a huevo trufado (a
soft egg yolk sitting in a warm, soft meringue and
speckled with black truffle); turbot served with its own
'crackling' and a nest of cuttlefish noodles, and much
more. The restaurant is sparely but elegantly decorated
with Murano glass on large, well-spaced tables, and
geraniums on a pretty patio.

Els Pescadors ★

Plaça Prim 1, 08005 (93 225 20 18). Metro Poblenou.
Meals served 1-3.45pm, 8pm-midnight daily. **Average**
€€€. **Credit** AmEx, DC, MC, V.

Full of Catalans showing their visitors just how good
local restaurants can be, Els Pescadors encapsulates the
best of modern and traditional Barcelona. One dining
room is beautifully old-fashioned, with marble-topped

tables, wooden chairs and dressers decked with spirits; the other is sharp-edged, red and steely grey. The dichotomy is reflected in the food; the emphasis is on superbly fresh, locally caught fish, prepared using age-old methods and given the occasional twist. A tuile basket of baby broad beans comes dressed with chocolate vinaigrette; cod is baked with honey and served with twirls of membrillo (quince jelly). An unmissable starter is the mejillones de roca con crema de puerros (mussels sitting in a dense soup of leek, carrot and onion) – a divine riot of flavour. Puddings are also wonderful, with lemon and ginger ice-cream on a bed of mango carpaccio or a fruit lasagne with warm chocolate sauce. Utterly fantastic.

Cafés & Bars

La Esquinica
Passeig Fabra i Puig 296, 08031 (93 358 25 19). Metro Virrei Amat. **Open** 8am-midnight Tue-Sat; 8am-4pm Sun. Closed 2wks Aug. **No credit cards**.

Els Pescadors

Horta & Poblenou

A comfortable barn of a place with dozens of wooden tables and a terrace out on the pavement, L'Esquinica is miles from anywhere, and always packed; it doesn't take a rocket scientist to figure out that the tapas here are hot stuff. Helpful waiters will advise first-timers to start with chocos (creamy battered squid rings), patatas bravas with all i oli, longanissa sausage and tigres (stuffed mussels). After which the world is your oyster, cockle or clam.

Oven ★

C/Ramón Turro 126, 08005 (93 221 06 02).
Metro Poblenou. **Open** 1.30-4pm Mon-Wed; 1.30-4pm, 9pm-3.30am Thur-Sun. **Credit** MC, V.

Dropped like a design experiment into the land that time forgot, Oven convinces flocks of glitterati that this post-industrial hinterland is the place to go for dinner or drinks. It embodies warehouse chic: acres of space, great sails lit with rainbow colours hanging from the ceiling, deep red sofas, fun house curved mirrors, and a high priest DJ spinning his stuff before an altar to religious and cartoon deities.

Hostal El Pintor in the Barri Gòtic *p31* has a branch at **Can Cortada**, Avenida Estatut de Catalunya s/n, 08035, Horta (93 427 2315).

The best restaurants

Abac
Xavier Pellicer's meteoric rise to superchefdom has dazzled the gourmet world. Catch him while you can (*see p97*).

Ca l'Isidre
The royals' choice. The finest of local produce and desserts to die for (*see p71*).

Gaig
Outstanding and owned by the same family for 130 years. Reader, we wept (*see p206*).

Jean Luc Figueras
Sumptuous luxury in the surroundings and on the plate (*see p160*).

Neichel
The very best of French cuisine in Barcelona (*see p189*).

El Racó d'en Freixa
Young chef Ramon Freixa turns out some unexpected delights (*see p163*).

Horta & Poblenou

GLOSSARY

Essential terminology

Catalan	Spanish	English
una cullera	*una cuchara*	a spoon
una forquilla	*un tenedor*	a fork
un ganivet	*un cuchillo*	a knife
un tovalló	*una servilleta*	a napkin
una ampolla de	*una botella de*	a bottle of
una altra	*otra*	another (one)
més	*más*	more
pa	*pan*	bread
oli d'oliva	*aceite de oliva*	olive oil
sal i pebre	*sal y pimienta*	salt and pepper
amanida	*ensalada*	salad
truita	*tortilla*	omelette
la nota	*la cuenta*	the bill
un cendrer	*un cenicero*	an ashtray
vinagre	*vinagre*	vinegar
vi negre	*vino tinto*	red wine
vi blanc	*vino blanco*	white wine
rosat	*rosado*	rosé
bon profit	*aproveche*	enjoy your meal
sóc	*soy*	I'm a
vegetarià/ana	*vegetariano/a*	vegetarian
diabètic/a	*diabético/a*	diabetic

Glossary

Cooking terms

a la brasa	*a la brasa*	charcoal-grilled
a la graella/	*a la plancha*	grilled on a hot
planxa		metal plate
a la romana	*a la romana*	fried in batter
al forn	*al horno*	baked
al vapor	*al vapor*	steamed
fregit	*frito*	fried
rostit	*asado*	roast
ben fet	*bien hecho*	well done
a punt	*medio hecho*	medium
poc fet	*poco hecho*	rare

Catalan specialities

Many dishes that are thought to have originated in other cuisines – risotto, canelons, raviolis, for example – are as entrenched in the Catalan culinary tradition as any other. Two names borrowed from the French, which frequently appear on Catalan menus, are foie (as opposed to fetge/higado or foie gras), which has come to mean hare, duck or goose liver prepared with liqueur, salt and sugar, and coulant – rather like a small soufflé, but melting in the centre.

a la llauna literally 'in the tin' – baked on a metal tray with garlic, tomato, paprika and wine

all i oli garlic crushed with olive oil to a form a mayonnaise-like texture, similar to aïoli

amanida catalana/*ensalada catalana* mixed salad with a selection of cold meats

arròs negre/*arroz negro* 'black rice', seafood rice cooked in squid ink

botifarra/*butifarra* Catalan sausage: variants include *botifarra negre* (blood sausage) and *blanca* (mixed with egg)

botifarra amb mongetes/*butifarra con judías* sausage with haricot beans

calçots a variety of large spring onion, available only from November to spring, and eaten char-grilled, with romesco sauce

carn d'olla traditional Catalan Christmas dish consisting of various meats stewed with *escudella*, then served separately

conill amb cargols/*conejo con caracoles* rabbit with snails

crema catalana custard dessert with burnt sugar topping, similar to crème brûlée

escalivada/*escalibada* grilled and peeled peppers, onions and aubergine

escudella winter stew of meat and vegetables

espinacs a la catalana/*espinacas a la catalana*
spinach fried in olive oil with garlic, raisins and
pine nuts
esqueixada summer salad of marinated
salt cod with onions, olives and tomato
fideuà/*fideuá* paella made with vermicelli instead
of rice
mar i muntanya a traditional Catalan combination of
meat and seafood, such as lobster and chicken in
the same dish
mel i mató curd cheese with honey
pa amb tomàquet/*pan con tomate* bread prepared
with tomato, oil and salt
peus de porc/*pies de cerdo* pig's trotters
picada a mix of nuts, garlic, parsley, bread, chicken
liver and little chilli peppers, which is often used to
enrich and thicken dishes
romesco a spicy sauce from the coast south of
Barcelona, made with crushed almonds and
hazelnuts, tomatoes, oil and a special type of
red pepper (*nyora*)
samfaina a mix of onion, garlic, aubergine and red
and green peppers (similar to ratatouille). Often
accompanies grilled meat and fish
sarsuela/*zarzuela* fish and seafood stew
sípia amb mandonguilles/*sepia con albóndigas*
cuttlefish with meatballs
suquet de peix/*suquet de pescado*
fish and potato soup
torrades/*tostadas* toasted *pa amb tomàquet*
xató salad containing tuna, anchovies, cod and a
romesco-type sauce

Carn i aviram/Carne y aves/ Meat & poultry

Català	Castellano	English
ànec	*pato*	duck
bou	*buey*	beef
cabrit	*cabrito*	kid
conill	*conejo*	rabbit
embotits	*embotidos*	cold cuts
faisà	*faisán*	pheasant
fetge	*higado*	liver
gall dindi	*pavo*	turkey
garrí	*cochinillo*	suckling pig
guatlla	*codorniz*	quail
llebre	*liebre*	hare
llengua	*lengua*	tongue
llom	*lomo*	pork
oca	*oca*	goose
ous	*huevos*	eggs

Glossary

perdiu	*perdiz*	partridge
pernil (serrà)	*jamón serrano*	dry-cured ham
pernil dolç	*jamón york*	cooked ham
pichón	*colomí*	pigeon
pintada	*gallina de Guinea*	Guinea fowl
pollastre	*pollo*	chicken
porc	*cerdo*	pork
porc senglar	*jabalí*	wild boar
ronyons	*riñones*	kidneys
vedella	*ternera*	veal
xai/be	*cordero*	lamb

Peix i marisc/Pescado y mariscos/ Fish & seafood

anxoves	*anchoas*	anchovies
bacallà	*bacalao*	salt cod
besuc	*besugo*	sea bream
caballa	*verat*	mackerel
calamarsos	*calamares*	squid
cloïsses	*almejas*	clams
cranc	*cangrejo*	crab
escamarlans	*cigalas*	crayfish
escopinyes	*berberechos*	cockles
espardenyes	*espardeñas*	sea cucumbers
gambes	*gambas*	prawns
llagosta	*langosta*	spiny lobster
llagostins	*langostinos*	langoustines
llamàntol	*bogavante*	lobster
llenguado	*lenguado*	sole
llobarro	*lubina*	sea bass
lluç	*merluza*	hake
moll	*salmonete*	red mullet
musclos	*mejillones*	mussels
navalles	*navajas*	razor clams
percebes	*percebes*	barnacles
pop	*pulpo*	octopus
rap	*rape*	monkfish
rèmol	*rodaballo*	turbot
salmó	*salmón*	salmon
sardines	*sardinas*	sardines
sípia	*sepia*	cuttlefish
tallarines	*tallarinas*	wedge clams
tonyina	*atún*	tuna
truita	*trucha*	trout

(note: **truita** can also mean an omelette)

Verdures/Legumbres/Vegetables

albergínia	*berenjena*	aubergine
all	*ajo*	garlic
alvocat	*aguacate*	avocado
bolets	*setas*	wild mushrooms
carbassós	*calabacines*	courgette
carxofes	*alcachofas*	artichokes
ceba	*cebolla*	onion
cigrons	*garbanzos*	chick peas
col	*col*	cabbage
enciam	*lechuga*	lettuce
endivies	*endivias*	chicory
espinacs	*espinacas*	spinach
mongetes blanques	*judías blancas*	haricot beans
mongetes verdes	*judías verdes*	French beans
pastanagues	*zanahorias*	carrot
patates	*patatas*	potatoes
pebrots	*pimientos*	peppers
pèsols	*guisantes*	peas
porros	*puerros*	leeks
tomàquets	*tomates*	tomatoes
xampinyons	*champiñones*	mushrooms

Postres/Postres/Desserts

flam	*flan*	crème caramel
formatge	*queso*	cheese
gelat	*helado*	ice-cream
música	*música*	dried fruit and nuts, served with *moscatell*
pastís	*pastel*	cake
tarta	*tarta*	tart

Fruïta/Fruta/Fruit

figues	*higos*	figs
gerds	*frambuesas*	raspberries
maduixes	*fresas*	strawberries
pera	*pera*	pear
pinya	*piña*	pineapple
plàtan	*plátano*	banana
poma	*manzana*	apple
préssec	*melocotón*	peach
prunes	*ciruelas*	plums
raïm	*uvas*	grapes
taronja	*naranja*	orange

Index

Ad Index

Please refer to the relevant pages for addresses and telephone numbers.

Metro
de Barcelona

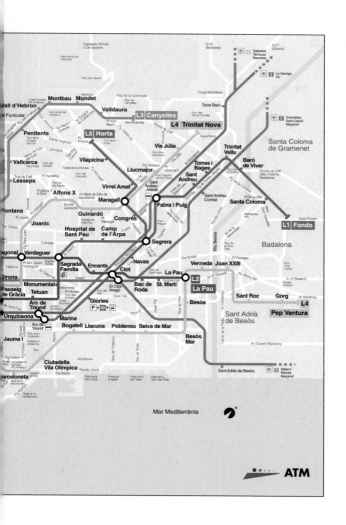

Barcelona by Area

HORTA (p204)

SANT ANDREU

AVDA DE LA MERIDIANA

SANT GERVASI

GUINARDÓ

Hospital de Sant Pau

LA SAGRERA

C/GUIPÚSCOA

GRAN VIA LES CORTS CATALANES

CLOT

POBLENOU (p204)

© Copyright Time Out Group 2002

RONDA LITORAL

1 km

1 mile

Plaça de les Glòries

Sagrada Família

EIXAMPLE (DRETA)

GRÀCIA (p156)

AVDA DIAGONAL

RONDA GENERAL MITRE

EIXAMPLE (p128)

PASSEIG DE GRÀCIA

C/ARAGÓ

PORTS & SHORELINE (p174)

VILA OLÍMPICA

PORT OLÍMPIC

Parc de la Ciutadella

LA RIBERA (p96)

Estació de França

PORT VELL

BARCELONETA

Plaça Catalunya

GRAN VIA DE LES CORTS CATALANES

BARRI GÒTIC (p24)

RAVAL (p68)

Catedral

LA RAMBLA

RONDA LITORAL

ZONA ALTA (p188)

SANT GERVASI

LES CORTS

AVDA JOSEP TARRADELLAS

AVDA DIAGONAL

PEDRALBES

AVDA DIAGONAL

AVDA PARAL·LEL

EIXAMPLE (ESQUERRA)

C/TARRAGONA

Plaça d'Espanya

POBLE SEC (p196)

Estadi Olímpic

MONTJUÏC

Estació Barcelona-Sants

SANTS (p196)

GRAN VIA DE LES CORTS CATALANES

GRAN VIA DE CARLES III

C/SANTS